A Mother's Song
How I Learnt to Praise Through Pain

by
Trudean Scott-Elliott

World rights reserved. This book or any portion thereof may not be copied or reproduced in any form or manner whatever, except as provided by law, without the written permission of the publisher, except by a reviewer who may quote brief passages in a review.

The author assumes full responsibility for the accuracy of all facts and quotations as cited in this book. The opinions expressed in this book are the author's personal views and interpretations, and do not necessarily reflect those of the publisher.

This book is provided with the understanding that the publisher is not engaged in giving spiritual, legal, medical, or other professional advice. If authoritative advice is needed, the reader should seek the counsel of a competent professional.

Copyright © 2016 ASPECT Books
ISBN-13: 978-1-4796-0655-9 (Paperback)
ISBN-13: 978-1-4796-0656-6 (ePub)
ISBN-13: 978-1-4796-0657-3 (Mobi)
Library of Congress Control Number: 2016900628

All Bible texts are from the King James Version unless otherwise stated.

Scripture quotations marked (NLT) are taken from the Holy Bible, New Living Translation, copyright ©1996, 2004, 2007, 2013 by Tyndale House Foundation. Used by permission of Tyndale House Publishers, Inc., Carol Stream, Illinois 60188. All rights reserved.

Scriptures taken from the Holy Bible, New International Version®, NIV®. Copyright © 1973, 1978, 1984, 2011 by Biblica, Inc.™ Used by permission of Zondervan. All rights reserved worldwide. www.zondervan.com The "NIV" and "New International Version" are trademarks registered in the United States Patent and Trademark Office by Biblica, Inc.™

Published by

"A woman is like a teabag; you can't tell how strong she is until you put in her hot water."

– *Commonly attributed to Eleanor Roosevelt*

This book is dedicated to God, my Savior and friend, and those here on Earth who are closest to my heart. Thank you.

I love you, Michael and Elianah.

CONTENTS

About This Book	7
A Mother's Pain	10
Aftershock	13
Penned For My Heart	19
My Journal (Part I): *Three Months Ago*	23
Giving Up Is Not an Option	28
My Journal (Part II): *Nine Months Ago*	31
Harsh Realities	38
From a Mother's Heart, Interview 1	41
From a Mother's Heart, Interview 2	43
From a Mother's Heart, Interview 3	46
Inside Research	48
Infidelity…The Marriage Stealer	48
Acceptance	51
Comfort	55
Praise Through Pain	59
Extraordinary Moments with God	62
Decisions, Decisions, Decisions	67
Weep Not	73
Hello and Goodbye	76
Epilogue: *10 months and 18 days later….*	80

ABOUT THIS BOOK

I have been pregnant three times; we lost the first, had the second, and lost the third. The first was within the first trimester and the third will be explained in the book. During the first experience of loss, I suffered great emotional and physical pain. I was still in the first trimester. As expected, I had to undergo a simple dilation and curettage (D&C) surgery to remove the fetus from my womb. That wasn't done properly, so I had to go back within that week to have the procedure redone. The physical pain grew to be even more agonizing because of the tenderness and the tools involved. Well, that didn't rid me of the remaining tissues inside me, so, I had to do it a third time. This time though, I flew to another country to have the procedure redone— hopefully properly this time.

This experience happened within two weeks. I was sore, uncomfortable, and in much pain. My husband, Chris, was very sympathetic and attentive. He really took great care of me. The trouble with having this done two times in one week was that I couldn't stop bleeding and the flow was too heavy to go anywhere other than the hospital. So, trying to fly to another country was challenging.

In short, the pilot and the passengers had to wait for me as I was stuck in a bathroom stall at the airport unable to put myself together in an approvable condition to fly. All the passengers had to wait as they brought my suitcase back to me in the bathroom. I was so grateful. I couldn't miss this flight, especially since I had a layover of a few hours in another country. This meant I could go into shock if not attended to soon. After I got a change of clothes and other necessities out of my luggage, it was brought back on the plane and I was gently escorted in a wheel chair on to the aircraft.

Everyone was concerned by now. I didn't mind. I was too grateful, and I desperately needed to lie down. I felt really weak and nervous. When we landed, I was taken immediately to the hospital for the third procedure.

Even as I write this now, I am shaking my head and holding back a chuckle, because I am amazed at my experiences and how I have come through them. Sure, worse came, but man, what a journey my life has been! However, nothing could *truly* prepare me for what was to come.

On a scale of one to five, five being the strongest, how strong would you consider yourself to be? True character, as most people know, is most evident when challenges arise.

When did you find out what you are made of? I'm sure you have had times where you had to pull something from deep within in order to cope and stay within your tolerant zone.

It can be a challenge to be understood and appreciated by others even when we are not in trying times. It is definitely true, that it is the "hot water" that causes others to see what we are made of. The process can be instructive, but it can also be discouraging for those who lack support.

When God created the first woman, she was made to be a companion to her husband and her role was a supportive one. I call her the "keeper of the flame." As such, she needs to be protected or covered. As I grew up, I came to realize that some women are very skilled at hiding, covering up, or bearing their troubles. Most times, one can never say what exactly is going on inside of her. Each family member should cherish the mother and wife as best as possible. Her duties are challenging and demand great care. (One informal survey showed that stores profited more on Mother's Day than Father's Day.[1] Now that I'm a mother, I can see why.)

During my second pregnancy, one of my more mature male friends counselled me, at one point, when I was feeling alone at one point. He said, "Women become mothers when they get pregnant, but men become fathers when the baby is born." I struggled to appreciate that, but later I understood why this statement is true.

Childbearing and child–rearing are not easy. Mothers are entrusted with a great—and sometimes frightening—responsibility: to carry a baby into this world as safely as is possible. Much energy and investment of time are needed in order to produce the precious, loyal, and productive people we all desire to meet and call friends. Most women endure at least some pain and discomfort during the pregnancy and childbearing process. (I myself counted more than eleven symptoms happening at once in my last pregnancy.) Many lose their entire body image, even more suffer extended periods of soreness, and some experience postpartum depression.

> *Pain is pain, especially this kind. Whatever it is for you, there is a need to share the hurt and to be held during whatever you are going through.*

Outside of medical reasons, people circulate their own personal theories get circulated as to about why women lose their child or children. The reasons don't matter: pain is still pain, no matter how it comes. Regardless of the choices that were made, no one should bear the pain of grief alone. For healing to take place, dependable support has to come from somewhere or someone.

It is a fact that some mothers bear pain alone simply because they have no one to turn to. This book was written with a deep, intense, and pure desire to point grieving women in a healing and saving direction. I have been writing this book in my head for some time now, but decided a few months ago to write it out for public eyes. As you read, you will be

---

[1] Linn, Allison. "Dad's not getting as much for Father's Day as Mom got for Mother's Day." Today.com http://www.today.com/money/dads-not-getting-much-fathers-day-mom-got-mothers-day-2D79778122. (Accessed November 4, 2015).

allowed into my private world through carefully selected journal entries. These journals, transcribed from the original writing, have the entry's date and time so that you can follow my timeline.

Whereas my story may not be as gruesome as others' stories, the pains are just as real as any other and the lessons are valuable. Pain is pain, especially this kind. Whatever it is for you, there is a need to share the hurt and to be held during whatever you are going through. Understanding helps to bring healing. I am truly sorry for whatever despair and pain you are experiencing right now. Life can be quite cruel at times and therefore, the future seems dismal and, honestly, sometimes pointless. Consider as you read through my darkest and lightest days that the process is very normal and know that I had help in God. None of my words or efforts woven within these pages would have existed if it were not for Him. The uplifting wonder of my experience is worth sharing with you. As you heal, you will in turn help others too.

This book is intended to save and restore lives like mine by extending an invitation for you to experience the joy in how I found my song.

A MOTHER'S PAIN

"Lo, children are an heritage of the Lord: and the fruit of the womb is his reward" (Ps. 127:3).

"My face is foul with weeping, and on my eyelids is the shadow of death" (Job 16:16).

I buried my baby girl today, Mother's Day—Sunday May 11, 2014. She lived for three months and one day. Her name was Elianah Valentina Elliott; the first name meaning "God answers prayers" or "God has answered." When I listened to my boss's tribute, giving the church the meaning of her name, I wondered again, *What did God actually answer? When will I know? As it stands now, I still come up blank.* Elianah's death was quite the shock of all our lives. We are still waiting for a divine explanation.

I was still on maternity leave when she passed away. Her three-year-old brother and I had come to visit their grandmother one week before her dedication service at my home church: the exciting plan we had come to fulfill. We had come home to dedicate her to the Lord, not to bury her! She died approximately twelve hours after admission on Wednesday, April 16, 2014 at 10:15 p.m.: a mere three days before her dedication service. Her cause of death was ruled as "congenital heart failure due to lower respiratory tract infection."

During the autopsy procedure, our church pastor stood by the window outside the morgue and overheard the doctors wonder aloud how it is was that she lived so long with such a large opening in her heart. You see, it was later revealed that she had a condition known as patent ductus arteriosus (PDA). The explanation the doctors gave was that, like fishes, babies use something like a gill function to breath in the womb, but the opening or duct normally closes within 48 hours after birth. It is assumed that this is a major reason that babies to cry immediately after being born. In my case, my baby was asymptomatic; meaning she showed no signs of defect. This was baffling to me, my family, and the physicians. We still don't know what kind of infection was suspected to trigger this tragic reaction.

It all happened so rapidly. She was put on oxygen shortly after we arrived at the hospital. She was admitted with a high fever, but giving her oxygen was more important than giving her a sponge bath. The attending pediatrician told us her heart was failing but the cause was unknown. He guessed that it was an infection. The x-ray result showed an enlarged heart confirming that something was causing her little heart to be overwhelmed.

My mother left the admitting room to wait outside as I watched my baby girl go through a spinal tap, urine sample withdrawal (a procedure which is carried out by a needle being inserted into the bladder to collect a sample), blood withdrawal, catheterization, and blood transfusion. Watching this was the *most* difficult pain I had to endure, but God was right by my side that entire time. I had endured two C-sections (one faulty), three D&C attempts in two weeks, and a marital separation caused by infidelity. However, all that paled in comparison to watching my tiny baby girl go through all that poking for hours on end, which was made even worse by the fact that the doctors could not find a vein for several hours.

I persistently made her aware of my presence by talking and singing to her. There was so much pain and anxiety when they began to close the curtains around her telling me to wait in another area. I ached to be right beside her.

I remember thinking aloud while my mother rubbed my shoulder vigorously, "How could God give her to me and then take her back?" Then a calm loving voice pointed out that God lost His child too. He lost Jesus. I responded to the voice, "But He got Him back! Jesus rose and God has Him again!" Then it dawned on me that that is my hope too, my proof that there is life after death. Jesus had to rise again to show us the power of God Almighty. "But if the Spirit of him that raised up Jesus from the dead dwell in you, he that raised up Christ from the dead shall also quicken your mortal bodies by his Spirit that dwelleth in you" (Rom. 8:11).

The doctors were still working hard to get her back to me. But, after thirty minutes, the leading doctor came to me, not knowing how to put it. With beads of sweat cascading down all over his skin, he began explaining the situation of how her entire system crashed when they began putting her on the life support machine. My ears were pounding so loudly that I could hardly hear the bulk of what he was saying. "She's not responding," he said, "but we will continue trying for another five minutes." They did—and that was the longest and shortest five minutes of my life. Even though the doctors had pulled the curtains, I was able to see when the monitor read zero. After pausing at the front desk, the pediatrician came back to me and sat beside me once again. He put his hand on my shoulder and said, "I'm sorry mommy, she's gone."

"NO!" I screamed. I raced to her bedside, but felt myself sink to the floor on my way there. I screamed her name, begged her to open her beautiful gray eyes, and called on Jesus for a Jairus or Lazarus miracle. "Please, please," I cried, in between, "open your eyes. Open your beautiful gray eyes, Elianah." Nothing made sense. *Why me? My baby girl is dead and I'm here, left to live life without her. Why?*

I wanted to walk away to preserve the beautiful living memories I had of her. I wanted to leave because she was already stiff, getting dark, and partially cold, but my heart couldn't pull myself away to leave my child on that table on which they had placed her earlier to get better access to her tiny body. Her brows were knitted and a blood-filled tube was coming out of her throat. *What happened?* When I finally tore myself away I ran straight back to her, crying the same things over and over again.

As I rested my head on her tiny chest, many questions raced through my head. *Why me? Why couldn't they stabilize her enough for her to be transferred to a better facility? Why now?* I kept listening for the monitor to start beeping again. It never did. I walked away with my hands clutching my sweater. "Thus saith the Lord; A voice was heard in Ramah, lamentation, and bitter weeping; Rachel weeping for her children refused to be comforted for her children, because they were not" (Jer. 31:15). A mother's pain is not strange to the heart of God.

Today, many people came to celebrate her short life with us. Many travelled from far places just to be by the family's side and I thank God for them. There were many sad faces, teary eyes, faint-looking dispositions, blank expressions, and some bearing hope. As the men covered her grave with cement, I silently reminded God to mark the spot where she lay. When all but a few were left at the graveside, I paused and looked out at the sea from that hill and said, "God, I am believing you. I am believing You."

What He knew I meant was that I am choosing to believe the hope of the resurrection, of life after this earthly life—after death. His Word says, "Marvel not at this: for the hour is coming, in the which all that are in the graves shall hear his voice, and shall come forth; they that have done good, unto the resurrection of life; and they that have done evil, unto the resurrection of damnation" (John 5:28,29).

AFTERSHOCK

"What time I am afraid, I will trust in thee" (Ps. 56:3).

In this life you can never tell what will definitely happen next or what will never happen. I had been away for about five years, and I hadn't seen my good friend since I had moved. It was good to finally get to see her. With outstretched arms, I almost ran to greet her. The embrace was familiar and welcoming. Oh how lovely that was! We pulled apart and began chatting, almost at once. We were so happy to see each other.

She told me she was glad I was divorcing Chris because, if I had asked her, she would have advised me against marrying him in the first place. Nonetheless, I was still enjoying the reunion until she said, "But you put on some size girl! You have to get back in shape." I was disappointed, but I let her finish, "You are young, you can't let it get away with you, you have to get back in control." What she didn't know was that I had recently promised myself and a another friend that I would tell the next person that talked about my weight exactly what was on my mind! But, she was a really good friend and, at that moment, I wasn't entirely in the mood to follow through with my promise.

I was quiet. As we turned the corridor of the university hall, I said, "You know I just had another baby, right?"

She looked stunned. "No! When?!"

"January." I responded.

"So where is the baby?" she proceeded.

"She died," I said dryly. "I just buried her in May, a few months ago." I believe she felt embarrassed then, because her face looked strange. I continued, "Which is why I look the way I do and I promised myself to tell anyone who comments about it exactly what is on my mind. People don't know so they shouldn't talk." Then I explained that I had another C-section and it was to be six months before I should consider robust exercise routines. Some recommendations even suggested that it be a year. I was peeved within because, once again, it had become clearer to me that physique impresses more than character. How does something like that come up in the very first conversation after being apart for so long?

This didn't happen just with her. It was infuriating. When I walked into my home church after having Michael three months before, many greetings included how my lovely figure had changed. I gritted my teeth many Sabbaths. Did they know I had a C-section? Did they know how hard it was to go through a fresh separation because of spousal infidelity? Did they know the level or depth of stress I was and still am under? I had to constantly remind myself that only the truth matters and that God loves me just the same. "The Lord hath appeared of old unto me, saying, Yea, I have loved thee with an everlasting love: therefore with loving kindness have I drawn thee" (Jer. 31:3).

Many other kinds of "aftershock" occur regularly. Just two nights ago, when I rushed with Michael to the emergency room, I heard familiar words that sent my mind reeling off into directions that were dangerously close to precious—yet frightening—memories I was trying to keep a lid on. As Michael lay sleeping on the bed, the attending physician said that he suspected Michael's symptoms were being caused by a lower respiratory tract infection. This was one aspect of his sister's diagnosis. After he stepped away to write a prescription and an x–ray order, I almost burst into tears. There I was, standing over my son in a hospital room with equipment and sounds that brought back upsetting memories.

> *When will this end? So many things were now creeping up or startling me into a place of anxiety, sadness, and impending depression. It felt so hard to climb out of this swirling black hole.*

I called my aunt and she anchored my emotions and gave me perspective. She has been a nurse for longer than my years on this earth. Her medical advice assured me that the two cases were unrelated and that his condition is not similar to hers.

When will this end? So many things were now creeping up or startling me into a place of anxiety, sadness, and impending depression. It felt so hard to climb out of this swirling black hole. I stared at the monitor as it beeped, and, once again, I had to fight breaking down. It was so very difficult—and still is. Many things threaten to plunge me further into an abyss on an almost daily basis.

Some of the innocent, unrelated, and related stimuli that can trigger for me this downward spiral include the following:

- beeping sounds of machines, phones, alarms, message alerts, watches, timers, games, etc. (These sounds remind me of the monitor that kept the time for Elianah's last hours on this earth with me.)
- baby girls that look like her
- pregnant women
- the scar on my abdomen
- movies about or with children
- my son's face (when they have a striking resemblance)
- scents from some laundry detergent
- certain songs
- hospitals

- "butterflies" in my stomach (this reminds me of her somersaulting in my womb)
- photographs in the house
- her hair clips and other baby items I saved (I have these placed in very visible locations.)
- the abbreviation "PDA," on vehicle license plates, in books, posters, etc.

Divorce was a shocker! I couldn't believe it had come down to this. Chris and I decided to separate during a counseling session when we saw that we were making no progress. Chris was tired of holding in his desire to smoke marijuana. I wanted no part of it, especially now that I was pregnant and Michael had bronchitis. This had never been an issue between us before; why should it be now? I was already trying to get over the "other women" issue, so this was far too much for me, and now a baby was on the way. When we discovered together that I was pregnant, he wanted to reverse his decision and stay. I disagreed. I told him, "Staying isn't a good idea just because a baby is involved." His staying would not have changed his smoking situation and his seeming need for "freedom." I am still waiting for answers.

God never intended that the union He blessed be torn apart by anyone. However, Satan's goal is to destroy our homes and, by extension, the church and society. Because of this, there are many broken people in the world.

I could never have been fully prepared for this aspect of the aftershock experience. Just the singular experience of grieving the death of my newborn girl was enough. That feeling alone was like being asked to braid strands from a cloud. By fair estimation, going through both life-changing and intense events like these two, at the same time, is unfathomable. Those of you who have had this happen to you and your family will know how difficult it is to live such a life for any period of time. An ever-thickening gloom, pressing sadness, piercing pain, loss of direction, and insatiable longing are just a few insufficient descriptions that try to tell what is felt in the soul. For me, most of it was too deep to touch.

I could not breathe. Nothing was fitting together. I was empty and hurt. Slowly, relief began to come with more effectiveness when I learnt the awesome truth of it all: Jesus is the way out of all the emotional clutter. Embracing this truth meant releasing all the doubts, pain, and fear. I desperately yearned to be free, so I made up my mind to hang onto the one thing I knew could grant me such freedom. The Bible bears another precious promise directed to us from the throne of God: "And the Lord, he it is that doth go before thee; he will be with thee, he will not fail thee, neither forsake thee: fear not, neither be dismayed" (Deut. 31:8).

Tonight, I laughed so hard I cried. That was refreshing and it lifted my spirits a bit. I was amazed at how I found happiness and reason to laugh at things that happened around me. My brother is one of those people who knows how to get to that emotion within me. He came for an extended visit and I have laughed more since his arrival than I have in many months. Even with the blessing of having him around to help me move on to a little higher plain, God orchestrated it all. I needed something and God gave it to me. It came in a different package, in an almost unexpected way. Yet, it was still His gift.

Sometimes we have to simply cast our cares on Him because He cares for us.[2] "Simply," I say, because it is simple. Tell Him, "Lord, I cannot handle this, please take it. Thank you for loving me." Then forget about it. It is no longer your problem—it belongs to God now. He bears the entire world; He can take your small one. Sure, you will feel hurt and sorrow at times, but now, look at it like this: you have to *feel* because you are human, but yet you can *trust* because you know God. "Consider the lilies how they grow: they toil not, they spin not; and yet I say unto you, that Solomon in all his glory was not arrayed like one of these" (Luke 12:27).

Physically, my body told the ailing secret within. My hair was in a disheartening state. Certainly a woman's beauty is in her hair. Hair is vital to our ensemble. Stress caused me to lose almost two-thirds of my hair from the root. I barely saved that one-third. What a visible aftershock! I was beside myself with worry and dismay.

One night, after washing and blow drying my hair, I watched as strands and more strands of it fell effortlessly onto the bathroom floor. Then, when I turned around to get a full view of my hair in the mirror, I was flabbergasted! Instantly, something rose up inside of me, swelling up and exploding into an outburst of stinging words. "Why am I losing everything? Why do I have to lose everything? I lost Elianah, I lost Chris, I lost my furniture, I lost my car, and now I'm losing my hair!" Then, with sincere frustration, I broke the comb on the face basin and flung the hair dryer with all my might. My friend saved it just in time. She tried to intervene when I was in my rage, but I swiftly evaded her and locked myself in my room—away from her and away from the guest she had brought over for dinner.

I was in no mood to be consoled or told cliché stories. I wanted the anger out. I wanted to express myself and I was tired of bottling it all up. "Why me? What did I do that was so wrong?" I asked once again. "How did I get here?" Then I went on in my head. *I've lost my beautiful figure and no one wants me now! Chris certainly doesn't seem to.* I was furious with God and the world. I sat on the edge of my bed and bawled—yes, bawled! The word "cried" would convey that there was some level of control, and at that time, I had none.

That night, after my girlfriend left, and after I was through shedding burning tears, I settled myself and called my sister-in-law. I wanted to be near that side of the family, and she is usually great to talk to. She answered the phone. The talk we had renewed my perspective and energy. I appreciated that call so much. We spoke for a long time and I was calmed and grateful.

Sometimes, when you hear someone else voice what is already in your head, you feel comforted or even empowered. She told me things I never knew that she thought and things that were frank and profound. When she told me how inspired she was just by how I handled the funeral activities and her brother, it made me realize that it was noticeable to others that God was carrying me. Then it hit home for me, again, that God really was carrying me through all this. "And even to your old age I am he; and even to hoar hairs will I carry you: I have made, and I will bear; even I will carry, and will deliver you" (Isa. 46:4). What a sobering thought!

---

2 (1 Peter 5:7).

Memories fade, and there is nothing a person can do to stop that. Some will be more vivid than others, but they all fade with time. Many memories may not die, but they all fade after a while. That is why the often quoted phrase "time heals all wounds" makes some sense. The memories of my little baby girl get so vague that it scares me. I fight many times to remember tiny details of her body, her coos, cries, laughter, gestures, and smells. I use her clothes to bring back to mind the scent detail. I still have the receiving blankets she died on. I never washed them, and, from time to time, I inhale the scent from them deeply. Sometimes, it makes me feel hollow, so I reduce the number of times I smell them. I play her favorite song on a toy that she liked to watch as she moved to the music.

I beat myself up for many things. I regret not using my camera to make videos. I made only two videos of her in spite of all the promptings I had within. I even deleted one because it wasn't a good enough quality. Now, we only have one forty-second of footage video, and, in it, she cooed once.

Soon after her death, I sent out a mass message begging for any videos or pictures anyone may have taken of her. I wanted to have it all on my computer. It was as if I wanted to be able to relive every moment she had with me through those pictures and videos. I was grossly disappointed that there weren't that many photos and that there was only one video. My son took a very short clip of us on the veranda the morning of the day she died, but her figure was in the background almost out of focus.

Painfully but purposefully, I made peace with my reality, even though I was dissatisfied that I had not maximized the use of our technological advancement to capture our memories. Initially, I watched that seconds-long video every night during my quiet time. I would play it over and over and over while I cried and smiled. Knowing that she will be saved in God's kingdom and having the assurance that, in faithfulness, I will hold her again took the edge off a bit for me.

I yearned to hold her, to look into her eyes, to kiss her cheeks, and to hear her voice. It was maddening to know that my longing was an impossibility. It was all so sudden. When we took her to the hospital, I did not know that she would never return home with us. Leaving her lying so cold and lifeless on that table bothered me as a mother for a very long time. The feeling is still inside me, but with less intensity.

The one regret I still have is that I didn't hold her when the opportunities arose after she died. I could have held her to my chest at the hospital and I could have held and kissed her in the autopsy room. Just the same, she looked so untouched and innocent. Because it was my first experience with death in this way, I didn't know what to do. Overwhelming emotions made my ears ring and my steps weak.

I wanted to hurry back and hug her when I left the autopsy room, but my friends held me back because they thought it would be too much for me, and they said they already heard the whirring of a machine. They tried to protect me from seeing anything I should not see as a mother. At the hospital, she was just lying there, stiff and lifeless, cold and dark. I kept rubbing my hands over her body and putting my face against hers, but I never picked her up. I should have. As I walked away from her body on both occasions, there was a tug inside to run back and hug her. I thought to myself, *She is gone, what's the sense? Why torment myself?* In hindsight, I wish I had returned to her side.

Now, I advise mothers and family members to hug the body as long as the doctors allow. Knowing that this is the final hug may help closure as you experience that final closeness. From my own experience, I encourage you to do whatever you feel necessary to help you to find closure. For weeks I walked around still clutching my clothes at the chest, in an effort to feel like I was holding her. I would hug myself a lot too. When I hugged and kissed my little girl, I didn't know it would be my last time. I have had to make peace with that.

Truly, it is an ideal privilege knowing God, our Christ, Savior and Lord. Such a blessing indeed! The power He holds over us is mighty to save and comfort. He is such a magnificent being. There is absolutely no one like Him. Job truthfully declared:

> I know it is so of a truth: but how should man be just with God? If he will contend with him, he cannot answer him one of a thousand. He is wise in heart, and mighty in strength: who hath hardened himself against him, and hath prospered? Which removeth the mountains, and they know not: which overturneth them in his anger. Which shaketh the earth out of her place, and the pillars thereof tremble. Which commandeth the sun, and it riseth not; and sealeth up the stars. Which alone spreadeth out the heavens, and treadeth upon the waves of the sea. Which maketh Arcturus, Orion, and Pleiades, and the chambers of the south. Which doeth great things past finding out; yea, and wonders without number. Lo, he goeth by me, and I see him not: he passeth on also, but I perceive him not. Behold, he taketh away, who can hinder him? who will say unto him, What doest thou? (Job 9:2–12).

He went on in chapter 37, to proclaim:

> At this also my heart trembleth, and is moved out of his place. Hear attentively the noise of his voice, and the sound that goeth out of his mouth. He directeth it under the whole heaven, and his lightning unto the ends of the earth. After it a voice roareth: he thundereth with the voice of his excellency; and he will not stay them when his voice is heard. God thundereth marvellously with his voice; great things doeth he, which we cannot comprehend. For he saith to the snow, Be thou on the earth; likewise to the small rain, and to the great rain of his strength. He sealeth up the hand of every man; that all men may know his work. Then the beasts go into dens, and remain in their places. Out of the south cometh the whirlwind: and cold out of the north. By the breath of God frost is given: and the breadth of the waters is straitened. Also by watering he wearieth the thick cloud: he scattereth his bright cloud: And it is turned round about by his counsels: that they may do whatsoever he commandeth them upon the face of the world in the earth. He causeth it to come, whether for correction, or for his land, or for mercy. Hearken unto this, O Job: stand still, and consider the wondrous works of God…Touching the Almighty, we cannot find him out: he is excellent in power, and in judgment, and in plenty of justice: he will not afflict. (Job 37:1–14, 23).

Our Lord is God of all the earth!

PENNED FOR MY HEART

"A friend loveth at all times..." (Prov. 17:17).

Tirsah flew from Trinidad to Jamaica to be with my family and me during our time of unbelievable loss. She was to act as "godmother" to Elianah. Along with her, came a heart-warming surprise—a little pink book with letters from friends and past colleagues of mine. This chapter is written to encourage people traveling down similar paths as I am. The words given to me are shared with the same deep sentiments so you can know that God listens and is concerned with your every care.

The cover of the inside page has a printed page taped on to it that reads:

Thursday, May 8, 2014

To Trudean Scott-Elliott,

From the hearts of friends, mothers and colleagues at the University of the Southern Caribbean, we extend words of comfort and encouragement to you on the passing of your baby Elianah. Revelation 21:1-4 (NIV): "Then I saw 'a new heaven and a new earth,' for the first heaven and the first earth had passed away, and there was no longer any sea. I saw the Holy City, the new Jerusalem, coming down out of heaven from God, prepared as a bride beautifully dressed for her husband. And I heard a loud voice from the throne saying, 'Look! God's dwelling place is now among the people, and he will dwell with them. They will be his people, and God himself will be with them and be their God. 'He will wipe every tear from their eyes. There will be no more death' or mourning or crying or pain, for the old order of things has passed away."

Thursday, May 8, 2014

Trudean,

My heart aches with you and I wish I could be there for you in so many ways, but I am happy that we can always stay connected in prayer. I am thankful for your life and the family God has blessed you with. I appreciate your friendship and love. I am blessed by you as so many others are. Let's see through to the end of the story my dear; because God is writing the pages of your life, I know it's a fabulous one. Keep the faith. I love you.

– Tirsah H.

Thursday, May 8, 2014

My Dearest Trudean,

This is just to say that my thoughts and prayers are with you. It is hard to take, but I trust that you would know the Master Teacher would never give you more than you can take. Besides, He will continue to give you the strength. May you be strengthened by the thought that some good day you will be reunited with your little "angel." Let us keep praying for each other.

– Franklin B.

Thursday, May 8, 2014

Trudean,

If my heart could be shared with you during this period I would share it. Since that is not how this works, I cannot begin to imagine the pain, yet, I am assured that God can and will cuddle your heart, mind and soul, not to understand yet, but to look forward to the day when you will hold her and kiss her again. May this day come. A big hug with a squeeze to you. May God strengthen you through this crucible. Love you and praying for you and your family. God bless!

– Judeth

Thursday, May 8, 2014
Trudean,

I heard of your loss, and have been trying to reach you a couple times and I was unsuccessful. I understand how you may be feeling. Remember God is in control even when we think He is not. Call or email me whenever you need to talk. We are here for you. Remember you are loved. Take care of yourself. Lots of love,
– Marsha H.

Thursday, May 8, 2014
Trudean,

I am lost for words, but the Lord knows how much you hurt. Be encouraged that there is a brighter tomorrow. You will never forget, but focus on the smiles, the beauty that God blessed you with. Only the Lord knows, but be cheerful to know that you have our support, our love and we will never leave your side. Joy comes in the morning.

Love always, Nordian S. & Family

Thursday, May 8, 2014
Trudean,

I know this is an extremely difficult time. However, I know that you know that no matter what, God is in control. Continue to trust God with all your heart and remember that you've got friends and family praying for you. Love,
– Marlene R.

Thursday, May 8, 2014

Hi Trudean,

You may not remember me, because I didn't work here with you, but we worked together in a Child Rights workshop. In this time of loss and grief my prayers are with you and your family, and your entire circle of loved ones. May your faith be strong and this is one time you religion must work for you. Be of strong faith and rest assured that God is still in control.

– J. Ragoonanan

Thursday, May 8, 2014

Dear Trudean,

My heart breaks for you at this time. I am weeping with you. I pray that one day this pain will pass and that you will be stronger for your experience. God knows your pain and is ever present to comfort. May He hold you in the palm of His hand.

– Rachael S.

MY JOURNAL (PART I)

Three Months Ago

What follows are some of the thoughts swirling through my head, three months ago, as it was a fight to find positivity and hope. I was scared and lonely and deeply in need of my husband. Yet, I was well aware of the new circumstances that would not allow us to be together at this point. I tried to keep my feelings to myself, so writing was my way of screaming and releasing what was in my head.

Friday, January 3, 2014

The doctor said all is well. I'm to get booked in on Tuesday, January 14 at 11:00 AM. Tears are in my eyes because I'd love to have Chris right there when I go in. I'd like him to be there, right through, just to be there! (Sigh.) Jesus knows.

Trying to get blood donors isn't easy! Only Chris has agreed so far. Imagine! (I was surprised.) He told me today that he hadn't smoked in approximately three months. I was so joyful inside. (As I understood it, this meant his blood would be safe for me to use.) I didn't say so. Maybe progress is being made after all.

My Auntie P sent clothes for the kids! Ain't that cool? God's name be blessed. She remembers me. She does.

Sunday, January 5, 2014

Ten days to go! Ten days before little baby Elianah shows up. I'm excited. I am not as perturbed about her care as before because Jesus is saving us all daily. That makes me happy.

Today I was sadly awakened to the reality that I cannot call upon Chris to assist me in any way. I toyed with the idea of asking him to come and be a full-time dad for a bit. But reflecting on the past year made me see that that would be a great disaster. He hasn't demonstrated any significant or consistent care for the family that he was instrumental in creating. It's all about him now.

The pressing thing is that I need a housekeeper during the healing period and a babysitter when I need to return to work in April. The trouble is that I cannot afford either. How will I manage? How will I make this work? Only God knows. … There is no money or any other support from Chris, their father. If I ask him, he may very well say no, thinking, "Trudy will fix it like everything else." (Sigh.) If only he knew the pain involved in getting most things done. He may say "yes," but then would probably give up and disappear again.

I feel so stupid and ashamed. I need your help God. Only You can provide and sustain. Only You can see beyond what I see in Chris and work on his heart. He needs You and I cannot help him find You anymore. He is my husband and only lover, father of my children. I do love him still and will open up if You bring him to me. Please help me to understand the difference, if there is one. Should you choose to do otherwise, please send the Holy Spirit to comfort and give strength and peace to move on. Thank You for answering my prayer. In Your Name I pray, Amen.

Sunday, January 13, 2014

I have to write something today. It's Sunday, two days before my surgery. I'm feeling less anxious about some things, but, at the same time, more anxious about others. Last week was my last week at work and, man, what a push that was for me! Moving around from bed to work, to meetings, to cafeteria, to meetings was just a real chore! I have been uncomfortable. There is much strategy involved in maneuvering such a huge body around. Sometimes I had to sit outside the office on a chair in order to breathe properly.

Yesterday, I peed seventeen times between 1:00 and 11:00 p.m.; approximately twenty times the night before. My nights have been less pleasant. Last week, I didn't have much success in resting while sleeping. I was either uncomfortable, crying, urinating, or having indigestion or nightmares. It is awful. Tirsah comforted me a whole lot. I used music to soothe my soul or I'd watch Golden Girls to laugh.

Chris did not give blood. (I shake my head.) This is so typical of him. What can I depend on him for outside of breaking my heart? He told me he got a week off, so, let's see…

…God has been merciful and has extended His thoughts toward me! Help came from family and friends in several forms. I am so humbled. More clothes came from Auntie P. I was driven to the store to get groceries for the house. Nicki washed and hung up two loads of clothes for me. Sasha fried fish for me. Blessings have come from all over. Last night, after almost nine hours of needing substantial food, Kaye and Sean came to take me to get something to eat. I called eight people that night. I almost cried. God kept the heartburn and gas away and that made the hunger more bearable.

Today, I rocked my way slowly through making porridge, sweeping, mopping, dusting, cleaning baby stuff, putting mats and carpet to sun, ironing Michael's uniform, and taking clothes from the line. My back burned. I paused a few times in between my household chores, especially when my heart began to palpitate in frightening rhythms.

I'm happy Elianah will be here! Michael will be happy too. There is a promise she'll bring or fulfill in this home or family, which I feel strongly about. She has all she needs right now and for that I am grateful.

Tuesday, January 28, 2014

Elianah Valentina Elliott was born by caesarean section on Wednesday, January 15th 2014, at 4:14 pm. at the Mandeville Public Hospital. She weighed 7.4 pounds and was 48 centimeters (18.8 inches) long—a beautiful healthy baby girl, another of God's children. Many friends came to visit; her father was there as well. I missed Michael the entire five days I was away. I'm so happy Mom was around.

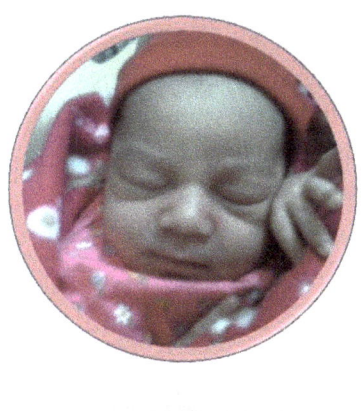

I came home to a welcoming party from downstairs. Everyone wanted to meet the baby that had made me sick, slow, heavy, and miserable. That was special. Michael's first act was to give her one of the toy trucks he had in his hand, then he ran for more. He was quite excited. I was pleased with his responses. He has been such a trouper. He has since held her, prayed for her, sung to her, helped to change her, etcetera. What a blessing! That's God's mercy.

When I came home with all that pain and fatigue, I was overwhelmed with joy at being home—my home. Such comfort. But then I was saddened because Chris was missing. I went into the bathroom and cried and cried. Folks were busy chatting and looking at the baby, so my cries were drowned out. I still felt incomplete. Pain was great and he would make it easier to bear.

Chris came later that afternoon and we had a small fight. Sigh. I cried to my brother on the phone. How could Chris want to leave me in that state in under one hour? Anyway, he stayed, massaged me, and took my temperature. (I had a fever of 101°F.) He ran to the store for formula because I thought my nipples would fall completely off or explode! He soothed me during that feeding. Wow! How awesome that was. Pain is so much easier to bear when you have love holding you.

> *Chris made my night bearable. He stayed with me on the phone last night when I couldn't sleep.*

I revisited the hospital twice: once for an allergic reaction to what we think was caused by Augmentin and one for terrible joint pains. It was not pretty. I was dealing with pains from the surgical cut and also from all my joints. Prior to this I couldn't stop shivering, no matter how warmly clad I was. I was shaking like a vibrating instrument. That was scary.

Today is not so bad. I've pretty much decided to cut the last underwear in the front middle to avoid squeezing the wound. There is a bit of sunshine, so it's not so cold. Elianah is asleep and I am about to be as well. Now she is fussing. Emotionally, I'm okay. Chris made my night bearable. He stayed with me on the phone last night when I couldn't sleep. That phone call was quite familiar, like an old pair of jeans. I hope that this is the beginning of something special and sweet. Many prayers are going up. Let's watch and pray.

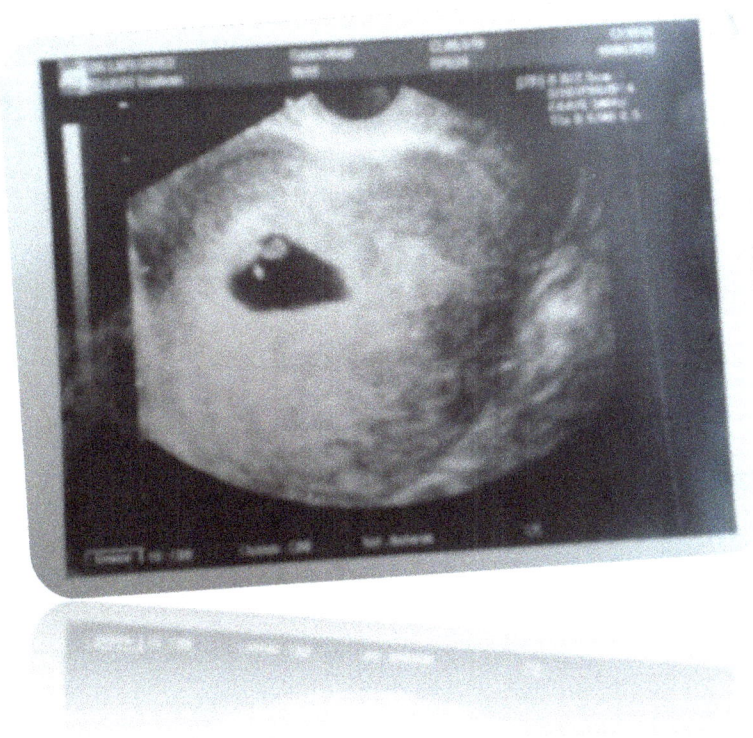

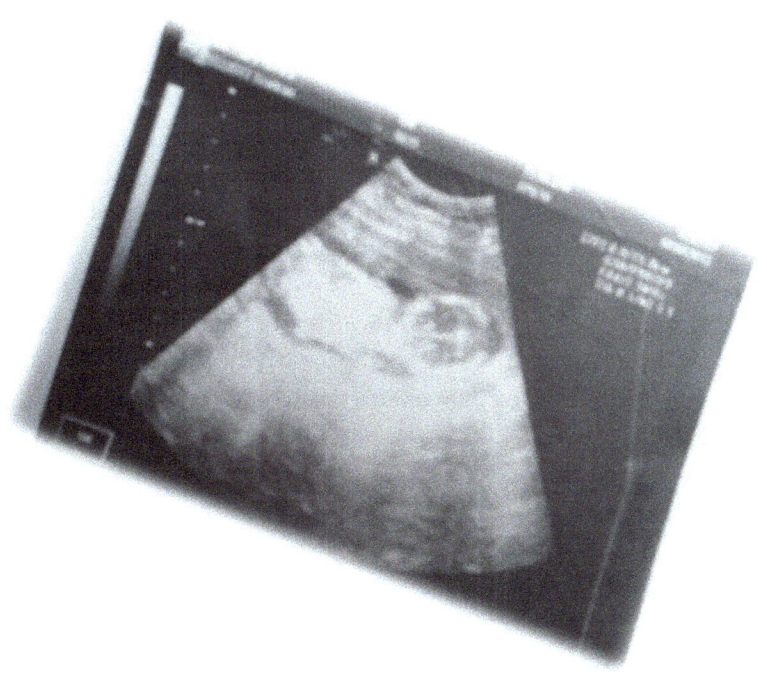

GIVING UP IS NOT AN OPTION

"He giveth power to the faint; and to them that have no might he increaseth strength" (Isa. 40:29).

My husband and I have been separated for approximately one year. It happened just about the time that we found out I was pregnant with our third child. Naturally, I was devastated. He was everything to me, but now with this split, it meant going through the second pregnancy completely alone. There were so many changes, so much misery, sickness, exhaustion, fatigue, physical discomfort, and, sometimes, pain that my entire world seemed to be capsizing. Sadness seemed to endure forever.

To be pregnant and alone is a horrible combination. Even though friends tried to be there for me, no comfort or assurance could compare to that which could come from the one closest to your heart, the one intimately woven into your being. The separation period had some really nasty episodes that made me realize that this was definitely not going to be a productive separation—one that would lead to reconciliation later.

However, 1 Corinthians 13:4 says "[Love] suffers long…" Though still separated, we were on talking terms when our baby girl was born. When she died, we were still separated. However, her death brought us to a place where we were talking to each other again and a sense of restoration was lurking near. I was nervous. I knew I could not take it if any issues that had blown apart when they were brought up before it reoccurred. My husband came to us the morning after she died. It was tense at first because I believed he should have been with me at the hospital when she was dying and we hadn't spoken much before this incident. As Providence would have it, we were thrown into a cordial relationship. Chris got really sick the day after she died and was admitted three days afterward, in the same hospital where Elianah died! You can imagine the level of shock and frustration. Here I was trying to handle the death of my daughter when another major incident blew out of control, and look who it happened to!

Now? Really? is all I kept thinking. But I knew it was not his fault. I couldn't imagine the stress level he was experiencing to make him fall ill so suddenly and critically. His condition was so severe that he had to remain in the hospital for a week and, when released, was sent home with an "at risk" warning. Chris is very reserved. He doesn't speak unless he absolutely has to. He doesn't share his emotions willingly so understanding what was in his head was a futile mission.

Oh, we were all so worried! He was almost down to skin and bones and we couldn't get a firm diagnosis. The hospital performed many tests. I would take the samples to the lab in the next town and bring the results to the doctor when they were ready. Many people, myself included, sent up prayers to God on his behalf. Once again, the church family proved faithful. There was constant concern about his well-being. We had reliable visits as well as other varied support. It was uplifting. Some would offer transport services while others worshipped with us, cooked for us, and checked daily on our needs—both at the hospital and back at the house. How pleased Jesus must have been to see His children fulfilling the law of Christ!

While Chris was lying in his hospital bed groaning in pain, I had to leave his side to identify the body of our daughter. This was the longest walk I had ever made. With my sister-in-law by my side, we started the dreaded journey to the morgue. My father and a few church family members were there to support and encourage. I was nervous, confused, hurt,

> *Tears clouded my vision and strange emotions swelled up and clogged my throat. My little girl was inside that van.*

sad, and struggling with hope. I had never visited a morgue before, so I had absolutely no idea what to expect. I wondered whether I would be able to go through with it. I pictured how she *might* look and what she *should* look like. I felt my body kick into survival mode and a fountain of strength welled up inside me. I was shaking on the inside, while supporters rubbed my shoulders and back I absent-mindedly felt their squeezes and heard people's whispers and nervous laughter.

Then the real experience began. The van pulled up, drove into the yard, and stopped. I cringed. Tears clouded my vision and strange emotions swelled up and clogged my throat. My little girl was inside that van. A few moments later, a tall dark stranger walked up with her strapped to a tiny thing that looked like a gurney without wheels. She was so tiny one could barely see her form without looking closely. I wondered for a few seconds if she was really strapped on under that green cloth. I felt strong arms wrap my body and I was able to remain standing.

I had a choice before me. I could scream and faint, or I could search to find an inner strength and live through this. It crossed my mind to give up. I was so in love with my baby girl. She and I were just getting to know each other, but, now, there she was—lifeless and cold. I cried inside for Chris. I wanted him to be right there with me. I was mad that he couldn't be. *Why? Again, why me?* When she was dying, he wasn't there by his choice. Now, at such a horrid time, he wasn't there because of something he couldn't control. Even though I knew this intellectually, it still didn't make the burden any lighter nor the confusion any clearer.

Just then, I decided to refocus my thoughts. The discussion began. The group and I decided to think of something to give back to the Lord in memory of Elianah. The hospital was a public one, and it lacked many resources. We contemplated, based on our experience, what kind of facility would make grieving people reflect on God during such a petrifying event. We thought of a church or a garden with covered seating or a paved and extended driveway. I left the morgue and headed back to Chris' room which was one ward away. I felt as if I was being lifted—carried to where I had to be next. The experience was still so surreal. Buried inside me were shattering memories that I would have to carry forever. Yet, somehow, I was still determined to make God seen in a tangible way.

The idea of getting back together as man and wife was quite short lived. Chris did not show up for the funeral, leaving both sides of the family in frantic wonder about his health and safety. A few days later, we heard from him. Needless to say, we were all grossly disappointed. That was the last thing we needed just then. How was I to handle my loss, a three-year-old son, moving on, with such actions from my husband?

The Bible reminds us to not be afraid or depressed about our saddening and sometimes maddening circumstances for God is with us wherever we may go. God promised to hold my hand through it all, and so, I depended completely on His grace. "… Be strong and of a good courage; be not afraid, neither be thou dismayed: for the Lord thy God is with thee withersoever thou goest" (Josh. 1:9).

I chose not to give up. I chose to cling to hope and not to cave in. I rested in the thought that God has a plan, and that His plan is never to harm me, but only to have me prosper in Him (see Jer. 29:11—13). I decided to be the living proof of God's miraculous saving and healing power. "There is point to all of this," I told myself and others. Elianah's death will save at least one life and Chris will be back with his family again.

Today, I am still choosing not to give up on God because He *will* never give up on me. Believe it!

MY JOURNAL (PART II)

Nine Months Ago

Monday, August 26, 2013

My son's birthday was thirteen days ago. The little money I had, I made sure some was put aside for that day. My son's grandparents—my parents—contributed to the day by buying him a gift I had seen that he would love. The cake was ordered, two gifts were bought, and Michael choose the ice-cream for his big day!

When August 13 came, it rained and rained. For a moment, it made me sad. The children who were invited could not come and that was disappointing (two were ill and the rain stopped the other). Anyway, the girls and I pushed to ensure that the day was splendid nonetheless. In the morning, we sang the entire "Happy Birthday" song, my parents called and sang, and the daycare made a beautiful poster for him. I missed a call from his other grandmother.

Michael was three—finally! He was so happy and quite aware of what the day meant. He ate cake, chocolate, and chocolate ice-cream. Then he opened his gifts: a baseball set, a tool set, and a golf set (from Aunty 'Dean, our neighbor downstairs). Michael danced and danced and played. Oh, he had good fun. I was broke now, but the memory created was worth it.

Unfortunately, his father called after he left for school that morning. Then he called again that night, about 8:45 p.m. Michael was not in the mood to speak with him then. Fortunately, Michael may never remember this neglect on his father's part. He never saw him that day and he didn't see him the day after the next one. Chris came on Friday evening. Michael had celebrated his third birthday the Tuesday before.

Chris saw Michael last Tuesday for approximately two hours at school and then went by his friend Romaine.* I'm not certain why Chris didn't stay longer, especially since he texted that he "wanted to see him." Shrug.

Chris told me he got a job! Terrific. I'm glad for him and relieved. I texted, "Congratulations on your new job. Do well."

He responded, "Thx."

Saturday, my phone rang. Guess who. Yip! It was Chris, wanting to see Michael. This was approximately 2:00 p.m. I said it was no problem and that he could come over. Well, again, today is Monday and he hasn't seen him yet.

I got another call from Chris. (Sigh.) I hate answering. It is just plain stressful. He wants Michael to live with him for some time in another parish. He asked me if I knew a school I could recommend. As if by reflex, I firmly said no to the idea. He got upset and hung up! (No strange thing there.)

Incoming text: "Y r u trying to deny me OUR son?! U don't have that authority in God's eyes."

Outgoing text: blank

I could have argued that he, in agreeable circumstances, kept himself away from "OUR son." Ha! I'm so mad and sad. What a text for such an action or lack thereof! He sees Michael for four hours at most when he does show up. Chris hasn't seen "OUR son" for twenty-four hours within the last two months. Where does Chris live? Fifteen minutes away, by foot.

I haven't told him that I filed for custody of our two children almost a month ago. The puzzling thing is why does Chris think he is fit to keep Michael for any period of time? Michael is not a toy, a meal, a thing, or a booster! Chris smokes and he is smoking something illegal. Michael is three years old and has respiratory issues! (10:55 p.m.)

Friday September 6, 2013

Since then, no word has been said about our unborn child. I'm not surprised—just sad that this is my reality. Sigh...

On Tuesday and Wednesday of last week, I sent my husband a text and an email (in that order) telling him of the custody filing I made about a month before. We all expected him to flip!

Nothing happened until Thursday at approximately 2:00 p.m. I do not wish to relive the horror, so the nutshell version will have to suffice. My husband barged into my office where I was hosting a meeting with my Administrative Assistant, and locked the door behind him, all in an obvious rage. It was frightening: all the swearing, banging, shouting, demanding, threatening, and attitude. Eventually, after my secretary left, totally ignoring his command to "sit down," she called the security personnel on the campus for assistance. They came to the door and

---

* This name is changed to protect privacy.

announced their presence, and then kicked the door in because my husband would not comply. Eventually, he opened the door and they guided him out, as I began crying. I packed up my things, and Michael and I slept away from the apartment for a few nights.

It is so sad. He walks too thin a line between freedom and imprisonment, sanity and insanity. He said he got a job in another parish, to begin September 2. So he's gone! I'm relieved but still cautious. Unfortunately, the court bailiff hasn't gotten a chance to deliver the summons.

Friday, September 6, 2013

On Monday September 2, Michael began his first day of school. I felt extremely proud. He is in Kindergarten! I still smile at the thought. What a smart looking boy. My mother bought his first uniform suit. I bought the rest. He is to get a P.E. uniform as well. ☺ The routine is hectic, but I'm managing. I'm praying for a car. So far, it's been four full days and he is enjoying it. He is quite adaptable. Today will be the last day of his first week.

Friday, September 20, 2013 4:00 AM

So, I'm only up because my son had a "night accident." The garbage stinks, I'll have to sleep in the living area and tolerate the stench. Anyway, as I tucked my son back into a clean, fresh, comfy bed, I had to pause and thank God. He is such an innocent and fragile boy with extremely great potential. Michael is sick now, but he'll get better with God's help. I will have to take him to the doctor tomorrow because his cough has gotten worse. It's consistent, especially at nights, and it is stubborn! (Sigh.) I honestly believe that God will provide and either of two things can happen—Michael gets a miraculous cure for his condition, or he and I will have to relocate. Either way, my Lord will fix the problem.

So, I chose a name for the little girl that has been reshaping my body and life. Right now, I'm seventy-five percent positive her name will be Elianah ___Elliott. Elianah means, "God answers prayers." This child has lived through several of those proof moments. Given the context in which she was conceived and born, her name is suitable. I'll teach her the ways of God and explain the blessings He has given her through this time.

I don't say much about her father because he has no presence in her life. For the first time in about six weeks he said something about her. He suggested a name, a name we made up a long time ago: Marley-Ann Danica Elliott. Later he texted that Valentina should be her middle name. Her initials would then read E.V.E.—like her mother, an affectionate name Chris gave me. He called me Eve because "life began when [he] met [me]". That's about all that happened on his part. No further communication has been done since that text four days ago. Yet, he says that he "cares."

I must say, for the first time in a long time I had fun—even during those moments, I was not completely into to the experience. After a long exhaustive day of concurrent meetings, the guys from the office brought me home, after which we bought dinner and played a game of UNO. Carla won! Poor Darren. I appreciated that so much because I only go out to get duties done. Plus, I am so sad all the time. Nadine and Carla made me laugh but they aren't my husband.

I'm really trying not to hate him. I resent him, wish he'd melt away, but, he's a soul nonetheless. (Sigh.)

Fifteen weeks to go! I have not bought anything yet (for the baby). God will answer my prayers again ☺ Good night.

Tuesday, October 1, 2013 10:22 p.m.

So, being called the 'b' word is absolutely no fun! Actually, his actual words cannot be written here because they are very unpleasant adjectives. This came about because he said, "I've stopped smoking…what else you got?" and I responded "Yea. And the Devil is sorry for all the havoc he caused on this earth. I hear you." I said it to mean, "When pigs fly…" He heard, "You are the devil." and told me that I knew that it would hurt and his response was quite in order. He said I deserved an equal response. (Sigh.) The little thread I had dangling between us just broke. I realized then that he does not love me and on top of all that, I have *never* been treated this way by any male before. The sad thing is, the person dishing it out is the one I'm married to.

Today he called for Michael, but Michael was asleep. He asked what my needs are, concerning the baby. I told him that I would email him the list. It sounds fishy. I still believe he is playing games. He has called for Michael the most times within a week. (Court is Thursday. He needs people to see a good picture of him, I suppose.) Chris still has the door and cupboard to fix. (Chris broke them in a rage.) I didn't think he was planning to appear in court on Thursday. He says I'll lose. He also says he needs to be invited to appear. I guess so. I've had enough of him.

Michael is doing extremely well in his development. He likes school and is trying to be autonomous. His vocabulary is growing rapidly and his receptive communication is impressive. What an imagination the child has! I am so proud of him. We try to have worship daily together. Each night I tuck him in, I say "Michael you are a good boy. You are a sweet boy. You are a smart boy. You belong to Jesus." It's so cute now because he says it with me. I'd like him to be God-fearing, respectful to all women, ambitious and thriving.

His sister is quieter. She moves much less than Michael did. I'm fine with that as long as it's not developmentally related.

There's just so much I need to accomplish with and for them. God will help me. Psalms 27:14 says "Wait on the Lord…" (10:50 p.m.)

Dear Jesus, thank You for my children. Thank You for the gift to carry life. Please keep them both with me and by Your side. I consecrate myself and rededicate them to Your will. Deliver Elianah into this world and into Your care. Make Michael a beacon for You. I humbly ask You to provide for their needs and remind me to tell them who sustains them. And Father, remember me… Amen.

Sabbath, November 16, 2013

Much has happened since we last spoke. It's now 26 weeks since conception and I'm still waiting to see God's work manifested in my husband. I heard from him today and, as with many other conversations, I was sad and disturbed afterward. It ended with him saying, "Have it your way Trudean, like everything else." This final statement came because he wanted to discuss the custody filing I had made and the information he received from his mom about a week ago, but I didn't want to "discuss" those topics on Sabbath. That got him upset. The thing is, I had hung up from a spiritually uplifting conversation with Auntie Pat and his line of conversation was taking away the spiritual high I so needed today.

It was a rough night—long too! Michael and I weren't feeling well. He got meds but I didn't. He coughed all night. He was restless. So, I was grateful for the "pep talk." When I called and related the conversation I had just had with my angry husband, she reminded me to see beyond the person and realize that the enemy is trying to make me forget the praise, lose the strength, and feel defeated.

Sometimes I wonder whether sitting down again with a counselor would do some good for us both. I believe he doesn't think I want to talk with him and the truth is quite the opposite. It's just that I don't want to speak with him in that condition. I still love him, but my needs are greater than what he can satisfy at this point.

One thing that happened this week was my being awakened by not being able to breathe. I couldn't breathe because, in my dream, I reacted as if I were living the experience. The experience was triggered by watching two videos that proved my husband's infidelity. Upon confronting him, he only said that he found someone new and wanted a divorce. His cold attitude broke what was left of my being. I was right there, at the same event, where the video was taken. I couldn't believe he could do such a thing, in public, with me only a few feet away. That hurt. I bawled in my sleep begging for answers, begging for resolution to my ongoing pain. It was too much to bear, so I had to wake up. When I got up, I took my Bible and read a chapter in Isaiah that spoke to God's promise for prosperity if we are faithful. I called Auntie Pat and told her about my dream and requested prayer.

On another note, to walk around (or rather roll around) and have people ask about my husband is silently embarrassing and painful. So many men treat me delicately and with great consideration or empathy because I am pregnant. While I appreciated their treatment, they made me sort of angry because I was receiving it from people I don't really know or with whom I have never shared any concerns. You could say I felt this because none was my husband.

I haven't received a penny from my husband whom God finally blessed with employment. He wasn't working for almost two years. I figured he needs a month or two of time to acquire a few things for himself. His work wasn't paying much but he still could have helped me some. This makes me so angry and I feel stupid.

Did I tell you Chris came up to visit Michael two Sundays ago? Yes. Chris came, took Michael, and brought him back, then left—all without entering the apartment. He didn't especially acknowledge me when I brought Michael's bag to him. He gave a general "bye" to everyone that was outside at the time and he said, "Food is in his bag," as he ran down the stairs into a waiting taxi.

This made me cry. He never really saw my tummy. He didn't try to converse. He didn't leave money for them and he never smiled at me. I've always seen this type of situation in the movies, but I never dreamed that my life would be witness to such a thing first-hand. It's strange to me, but not to him.

Naturally, I had to deal with a roller coaster emotional child after his visit. Now Michael asks, "Where's my daddy?" or he says, "I want to show Daddy."

I'm going to lie down now. I'm tired. I have a headache. I'm sad. Plus I have to go check on Michael because he keeps coughing.

Wednesday, November 21, 2013

If I allow how I feel to reign, I'll never write. I get so tired after work. Most times, it's so powerful and overwhelming that all I want to do is cry. I want to cry, but often don't, because I really want to rest and cuddle with my husband. Pray as hard as I might to Him, Jesus won't come down and be beside me physically, so I can lie down on His chest and sleep. (Sigh.) I wish that so many times.

What I really want to pen today is about my blessings! God has been there for me right through all this madness. Because funds are really low, I cannot eat as often as my system indicates I should. However, on two really special days, because I was really hungry, J. gave me substantial snacks (bun and cheese)[3] to eat. Man, I felt so awesomely blessed. God's Name deserves glorification.

Monday December 2, 2013

I hugged my tummy and cried and cried and cried and cried. I cried so hard today that the baby was disturbed in an unusual way. Not a good way to start the Christmas season at all. The last thing I needed was to have my husband confirm my fear of his cheating on me and then to hear from his mom that she supports the action because we are "separated." When did separation make married people single? What is going on in this world? To think I was considering a reconciliation! (Sigh.)

Just last night he told me that we are one flesh and that he doesn't want a divorce. Ha! That is such a joke. I want something special—for me. I don't want

---

3 "Bubble and Squeak." Wikipedia. 30 Oct. 2015. https://en.wikipedia.org/wiki/Bubble_and_squeak. (Accessed November 4, 2015).

what the world vomited up and tries to give me. My children and I deserve better than that.

It's now 5:00 p.m. and Michael will be here any minute. I have to find some way to keep control of a haughty spirit, as he needs me. He's going through so much. Poor child. He's such a darling. My newest ring tone is of Michael singing "My God is Awesome." So cute!

Chris is here! It's show time!! May God help me.

Tuesday December 10, 2013

He called tonight to speak with his son, of course. He has been calling more since the conversation we had when I recommended that he call Michael *every day!* After talking to him via speakerphone, because Michael wasn't interested in talking, he asked me how the baby was, how I was doing, specifically, and how Michael's moods have been of late. That was a shocker!!! He sounded sad and he had a longing in his voice. Hmm… What does that mean?

HARSH REALITIES

"Thou art my hiding place; thou shalt preserve me from trouble; thou shalt compass me about with songs of deliverance" (Ps. 32:7).

I am afraid. I have been afraid of opening this saved document to put my thoughts on paper. My reality is harsh. Honestly, I'd rather not write, but I made a promise—a promise to do God's work. Even as I write, I wonder if this is the purpose, the burden placed on my heart by God. I cannot bear reliving each moment as I type. The faces, the coldness, the anger, the hate, the death, and the fear of everything can get pretty overpowering.

I am sitting with a humped back on my bed, knowing that I further risk aggravating an already annoying and painful situation. Last month, I was back in my neck brace because my spine began to hurt again. In February 2013, I was diagnosed with cervical kyphosis: in layman's terms, my cervical spine is turned in a backward "C;" so technically, I am supposed to be holding my head in the upward position, not looking down at the laptop. I should buy a work desk, but I have to wait on affordability. Medical bills are quite expensive, especially since on Thursday I was clinically diagnosed by a psychologist as "depressed." Ha! What a surprise.

Dealing with my baby girl's death, a nasty divorce, a 4-year-old son with bronchitis, my spine issues, our relocation, my new boss, and settling into a house to make yet *another* home is blinding and arduous. I often pray within that God will relieve me of a few of the pains. Sometimes it's like He is absent.

Have you ever watched a movie and seen "two years later" or "six months later" flash across the screen in the midst of a crisis? Time just flew right by our eyes. It's like the screen writer said, "Yeah yeah, blah, blah, blah." The next scene usually follows up with a well-adjusted protagonist or "star" emerging successfully after going through all the phases of failure or hurt. I often wish that would happen in my life. Have you ever wished that? I have wished that I could go to bed after a horrible experience and wake up the next morning to a well-deserved stretch, with a chirpy attitude, and a new life outside my bedroom door. Honestly, I could use a "five years later" kind of script. Life seems to just drag on and on and on and on.

Folks kept saying, "God won't give you more than you can bear." That doesn't help. It only makes Him seem more cruel. How can He watch me go through all this in the *first* place, then for such a long *time*? How much more will He take from me? What did I do to be punished so harshly? Does He really mean that He wishes that above all things I be happy?[4] Well then, when is it my turn? In my culture, we have an old but wise saying: "Not everyone eats breakfast at 9 o'clock." Tonight, when my sister called to give me her motherly talk and sisterly inspiration, I confessed my thoughts. I said, "I know not everyone eats breakfast at 9 o'clock, but gosh, for me it's like 7: 30 or 8:55, 8:55, 8:55 all the time... It's never 9:00! When will *I* smile?"

Soon after Elianah died, I came upon a book written by Joy Swift, entitled, *When Death Isn't Fair*. It was just sitting there in my mom's library waiting patiently for me to find it. When I asked if she strategically placed it there for me, she said she had not. Anyway, it was there and I was grateful. In the book, the author tells a horrific story of how both she and her husband lost all five of their children within a month. While out at dinner, they lost four to murder by one of their sons' playmates, who shot them to death one night. The youngest child was 17 months old. More tragedy struck 28 days later. Their first child died from cancer. What is the proper response after reading something like that when it happens to someone as normal as you?

Sometime later, I saw a news flash displayed across the MSN screen: "Body of infant abducted from California home found."[5] The infant was only three weeks old and her parents and another adult in the vehicle were shot and wounded. Hopelessness and despair only vaguely described my emotions when I saw that headline. Not knowing where your child is must be torturous. It would be just too much pain.

This type of loss and pain is real and common in some parts of the globe. Tragedy snatches people away in gruesome manners at the blink of an eye and is even more painful, I believe, than natural or sudden loss from health issues. Take Bill Cosby's loss of his son. ABC News published on February 9, 2014 that, "The man convicted of killing Bill Cosby's son has confessed to the murder and withdrawn the rest of his appeals."[6] On January 16, 1997, Mikhail Markhasev murdered Ennis Cosby. Ennis was shot to death in a robbery attempt while attempting to change a spare tire.

Who knew? Why did it happen? Death isn't biased; it touches all levels of society. Celebrities, outstanding Christian men and women, and common people all face the pain of death sooner or later. There is an unfortunate misconception that people who experience this depth of loss are far away from God or that they are being punished for something. The truth is that bad things *do* happen to good people. Satan intends to destroy all humans alive. Therefore, he will get to us in one form or another. Some have easier trials than others. Nevertheless, sin touches everyone. It is only in keeping in touch with God

---

4 (3 John 2:2).

5 Associated Press. "Body of infant abducted from California home found." MSN.com. 5 Jan. 2015. http://www.msn.com/en-us/news/crime/body-of-infant-abducted-from-california-home-found/ar-BBhvwKO. (Accessed November 4, 2015).

6 Robinson, Bryan. "Convicted Killer of Ennis Cosby Confesses." ABC News. 9 Feb 2015. http://abcnews.go.com/US/story?id=94100. (Accessed November 4, 2015).

and asking for His protection and grace that we are able to sustain ourselves through our disappointments and hurt. Remember, "Many are the afflictions of the righteous: but the Lord delivereth him out of them all" (Ps. 34:19).

From a Mother's Heart, Interview 1

Here is a story I could touch. I did not read it in a book. It happened to a well-esteemed colleague of mine where I worked at the time I wrote it down. She shared her story when she mustered up the strength to approach me after hearing about my loss. I asked whether she would be willing to have an interview with me. The following is what we said:

Q. Though the situation is quite sad, it is a relief to hear other stories like my own. It made me feel like I was not alone in dealing with such a horror! Tell me, how old was your baby when he or she died?

A. *My twin babies died at different ages: Baby #2 (a girl) died two days after birth. Baby #1 (a boy) died six months after birth.*

Q. You don't need to give me great detail, but please share how it happened.

A. *Both deaths were due to complications caused by prematurity and Jamaica's lack of trained pediatric doctors, nurses, and newborn intensive care units.*

Q. It must have been a jolting experience for you. How in this world did you manage to cope with that kind of pain?

A. *Coping with the pain was very difficult since my previous pregnancy also delivered prematurely (approximately six weeks earlier in pregnancy than the twins), though that child is alive and well today. I did not expect any of this since the twins were at a much more advanced state of gestational maturity. My only daughter died (I had two boys previously), did not stand a chance as practically no effort was made to help her. However, I called on my "Burden Bearer," my Rock, my Shield and Stay, my Comforter, the One who never leaves me nor forsakes me.[7] He kept me sane and standing tall. He helped me to bear my pain. I thought that the loss of my daughter was devastating, until I lost my son. Such pain I never felt before, and I hope and pray that I never will again! However, the Holy Spirit showed me that there were lessons in this experience that I needed to learn and not until I realized this and asked God to help me to learn these lessons, did I truly begin to heal.*

---

7 (Deut. 31:6–8).

Q. If you can, tell me what your greatest feeling of regret was and is? It doesn't necessarily have to be about the baby, but perhaps the situation or experience in general.

A. *My greatest feeling of regret is that I did not learn the lessons before. The Lord had to "bruise" me in order for me to hear His voice and follow His leading. He wanted me to help people in a major way and I had allowed myself to get caught up in other things while people and souls were hurting and needed my help.*

Q. What can you tell us to make our experience more bearable?

A. *Take one day at a time. Lean heavily on God's promises. He will never, never leave us nor forsake us.[8] Nor will He give us more than we can bear. So in it all, we should learn to ask: Why is this happening to me? What lessons does He have for me to learn? How can I use this experience for good and not allow the devil to break me down? God is our "Way-maker" and "Chain-breaker." We can do all things through Him because He strengthens us.[9] In Him we have our strength, in Him we live and move and have our being,[10] and He does not want anything to happen to us to hurt us. He loves us too much. So whatever is happening in our lives must be for a reason—we need to find out what that reason is. We need to listen to His voice, whether it is booming or whether it is a still, small voice.*

Her advice is that it is also ok to cry whenever you feel sad. This is human, and tears are a great healing agent. Don't ignore the fact that your baby or babies existed. This will not help anything. Talk about him or her, cry, laugh, heal, and in everything, give God thanks! He is Alpha and Omega, He knows why he allows certain things to happen to us. In everything we should give Him all the glory.

– Alana*

---

8 (Deut. 31:6—8).

9 (Phil. 4:13)

10 (Acts 17:28).

* This name is changed to protect privacy.

From a Mother's Heart, Interview 2

When I relocated to Trinidad, I told my story in church during a testimony worship program. Afterward, it came to my attention that one of my colleagues, whom I worked with for many years when I was living in Trinidad before, had gone through a similar experience. When I asked her if she would be willing to share her story to inspire other women like us, she accepted with joy. This is her story.

Q. Though the situation is quite sad, it is a relief to hear other stories like mine. It made me feel like I was not alone in such a horror! Tell me, how old was your baby when he or she died?

A. *My baby was just five months old when she died.*

Q. You don't need to give me great detail, but please share how it happened.

A. *It all happened in the year 2005 when my husband and I were teaching in a Seventh-day Adventist College in a state called Surat in India, where my second daughter, Sanna, was born on the 14th of May 2005. After her birth, as it was a custom, I went to my parents' home in another state called Hyderabad to spend the remaining days of my maternity leave.*

It was during that time that we had a big flood from heavy rains, and the breaking of a huge dam in Surat caused many houses including ours, to go under water. It was God's leading that sent my husband out of Surat on his way in a train to Hyderabad to bring us back home. We were informed about the flood and told not to return until we were advised to do so. My husband returned after a week. Seeing the condition of the area and our house, my husband asked me to remain at my parents with the children, as it didn't seem very safe—especially for the new baby.

I returned two months later. A few weeks after I returned, the baby got a fever. We took her to the doctor and, in spite of giving her medication, the fever didn't leave completely. I remember sitting up the whole night giving her sponge baths. Early the next morning, we carried her to the doctor again and told her that the medication was not working. I remember the words of the doctor clearly: she said, "It's medicine, not magic. It's a viral fever and will take five to seven days to leave. Continue the same medication." As worried parents, we were not satisfied, and we got an appointment with another doctor in a different hospital. Unfortunately, the appointment was for the following day.

By that evening, in spite of giving her medication and the sponge bath, the fever went very high, so we rushed her back to the first doctor. Even though she knew that our baby had a very high fever, she still took her time attending the other children because they had been there before us. When we got our turn, the nurse was asked to give our baby a sponge bath and then we were sent to get a blood test done. Sanna didn't cry at all when she was pricked, and we just thought she was a brave and strong baby, as most babies cry upon being pricked.

While walking back to the doctor's office behind my husband, I noticed a strange look on the baby's face. Her face started to turn blue and her head turned in to one side. I knew something was happening, and I shouted to my husband that something was happening to the baby. We ran into the emergency room just few steps away. The nurses took her from us, and she started to have convulsions. They pushed some tubes down her nose or throat—I really don't know which they were because I was in complete shock! The doctor came in after a few minutes and she told us to carry her to the children's hospital because they didn't have certain necessary equipment.

Our baby was rushed to a special hospital for children where she stayed for four days. Many doctors checked her, doing all kinds of tests and they told us that only 20% of her heart was functioning. Her brain and liver were also not functioning well. There was seemingly not a place on her body that was not pricked by a needle. She even had needles in her head and feet. After she was on the ventilator for four days, I lost my baby on October 30, 2005.

Q. It must have been a jolting experience for you. How in this world did you manage to cope with that kind of pain?

A. *While she was in the hospital, we had lots of friends and family around us, and our church members were praying for her. Many of them came to visit her. There were many prayers offered around her bed. Many of our friends and relatives who were overseas who could not come talked to us over the phone. The truth is that I never thought that I could lose my baby. I believed that she would get well soon. I kept telling everyone who tried to console me that nothing would happen to her. I kept having my personal prayers, and I felt 100% sure that my God would make her well. Moreover, almost everyone I knew was praying for her—even little children. How could God not answer? I was strong and confident.*

It was only when the doctors told us that our baby was no more that I broke down. I just couldn't believe that God would allow something like that to happen to me! But trust me, no matter how painful the pain may be, God gives us the strength to go through it.

"There hath no temptation taken you but such as is common to man: but God is faithful, who will not suffer you to be tempted above that ye are able; but will with the temptation also make a way to escape, that ye may be able to bear it" (1 Cor. 10:13). Though I still have many questions about why God allowed such pain, I trust Him and believe He knows the best for us. I also know that all my questions will be answered when I get to Heaven. One thing that really comforts me is that my baby, being sinless and pure, will surely enter the gates of Heaven. My desire to see her and hold her in my arms again makes me put forth extra effort to live a life that is acceptable in the sight of God.

Q. If you can, say what your greatest feeling of regret was and is? It's not necessarily about the baby, but perhaps the situation or experience in general.

A. *My greatest regret is of the bitter feeling I had against God. I was so angry with Him for allowing a baby—a sinless and innocent baby—to lose her life. I wondered why God would give her to me in the first place if He had to take her away. You see, I had lots of complications during and after my first delivery. I was prescribed bedrest with medications for almost nine months after the delivery. Then I conceived even before my first child's first birthday. Due to my pain and other complications, my doctor told me to abort the baby. I believe a child is a gift from God, and thought that even though it was only as big as a seed, it had a heart and life. I refused. I didn't want to kill my baby. Going against the doctor and family, I kept her. With great struggle, I carried her in my womb for nine painful months. You can't imagine the joy I had when I held her in my arms!*

In spite of all I went through, why did He let this happen? I was so angry, that I even stopped praying and talking to God for months. When I look back, I am ashamed of my negative feelings toward God.

Q. What can you tell us to make our own experience more bearable?

A. *Well, I would just like to remind everyone of the story of Job. In spite of all he lost, he said, "Naked came I out of my mother's womb, and naked shall I return thither: the LORD gave, and the LORD hath taken away; blessed be the name of the LORD" (Job 1:21).*

God has plans for us that we can never fully understand. Yet, we need to trust Him. I have already said, our babies, being sinless and pure, will surely be in Heaven. Maybe God does not want you and me to be left behind on that Great Day, and now we have a greater reason to be there, don't you think?

–Anupama

From a Mother's Heart, Interview 3

Q. Though the situation is quite sad, it is a relief to hear other stories like mine. It made me feel like I was not alone in such a horror! Tell me, how old was your baby when he/she died?

A. *My baby girl, Kenyan Kayleigh Maria Bramble, was one year and a few days old.*

Q. You don't need to give me great detail, but please share how it happened.

A. *She was born full term via C-section but had a congenital heart defect that needed surgery to correct. We went abroad for help, but by the time we got it at seven months, she was too sick for surgery—her lungs were too damaged. So, we came back home in October, and she died in March of the following year.*

Q. It must have been a jolting experience for you. How in this world did you manage to cope with that kind of pain?

A. *The pain was and still is strong. The most pain I felt was when I received the diagnosis. Her actual death was a mix of relief and sadness because it meant the end of her suffering. I coped with the pain by what the pastor said at the funeral—that she will be saved if the parents are saved. Also, at the wake, another pastor told me that I was chosen by God for this experience even before I was born. I also cried a lot. One day I cried until I could barely breathe.*

Q. If you can, say what your greatest feeling of regret was and is? It's not necessarily about the baby, but perhaps the situation or experience in general.

A. *Regrets? I don't have regrets, just thoughts of "what if," like, What if I didn't get married? What if I had better prenatal screening? I also had the crazy thoughts of killing her and my son. That was my lowest point after the diagnosis.*

Q. What can you tell us to make our experience more bearable?

A. *To make it more bearable? I don't know. For me, the doctrinal beliefs of the church about death and resurrection of babies made it more bearable for me. I also prefer that she is asleep and not alive suffering with an illness.*

-Lizzi[*]

* This name is changed to protect privacy.

The most admirable quality I find about Jesus is that He never ever gives up on His children. The Bible does give a calming assurance in 1 Corinthians 10:13 as my colleague Anupama mentioned in her story. God is faithful. He knows my heart, but it can be so mixed up, and sometimes, my mouth goes before my heart. Moreover, even though He hears me lament, He still speaks with the gentlest of voices. Sometimes I wish I could hear Him bellowing directly to me from the clouds. I would wish this, but, ironically, He actually *does* do it. It may not be His voice per se, but His creations, providential events, and miracles are mediums of His communication. We should listen. His speaking in thunderous tones from the sky would get kind of boring after a while, wouldn't you say? Knowing us humans, we'd probably say, "Yea, yea, I heard you the last three times…I'm coming!"

Job was an amazing man. Job had the story of a lifetime—literally. All his life investments were snatched away in a single day. His livelihood, children, and servants were all destroyed in a few hours. As a matter of fact, he had hardly heard each piece of heart-wrenching news before the next messenger came running with more. It is a tragic story, created in one day. What did Job do or say? "Then Job arose, and rent his mantle, and shaved his head, and fell down upon the ground, and worshipped, And said, Naked came I out of my mother's womb, and naked shall I return thither: the LORD gave, and the LORD hath taken away; blessed be the name of the LORD. In all this Job sinned not, nor charged God foolishly" (Job 1:20–22).

It sounds crazy, right? Or, it sounds like he never actually worked for any of the things that he lost. Why was he so calm? It was because he had the peace that is only found in trusting God. Until you have experienced His peace personally, it will seem like an exaggerated fable. Put your will into His hands and experience the calm for yourself. No matter the type of pain, it is possible to heal with great success.

The next chapter introduces a topic of another harsh reality that I had to face and accept. I had buried it for so long. With all this new pain, my heart was bursting from the inability to hold both sources. This is a common pain that many women experience, but even in this one, healing can be found.

Let me leave this thought with you and pray for your consolation as you walk your own journey through a sometimes unfriendly and hurtful world. "Blessed be the God and Father of our Lord Jesus Christ, which according to his abundant mercy hath begotten us again unto a lively hope by the resurrection of Jesus Christ from the dead" (1 Peter 1:3).

Don't forget, *all* things are possible with Christ—believe it. Claim your healing and embrace a beautiful hope.

INSIDE RESEARCH

"But whoso committeth adultery ... lacketh understanding: he that doeth it destroyeth his own soul" (Prov. 6:32).

My pain is compounded by having to handle the separation of my husband and me. Our marriage was in a terrible state and I felt seriously alone and lost. The one and only person I needed to help me through this and to be with me in all of this made himself unavailable. Many mistakes and indiscretions caused our family to be torn apart. We had tried to make it work, but there were bitter consequences and so much hurt that kept it from being as smooth or tolerable for us.

Some of you may be experiencing or may have experienced strikingly similar situations and know that it is not easy. Others may have a portion of what I experience or additional factors that make grieving next to impossible. Do not give up!

When my girlfriend, Tash, told me about her research, I asked her to share the scientific insights and conclusions with my readers. It was very important to me because I was not convinced that the betrayers truly understand the concept. Those who commit themselves to an adulterous life and those who seek after married partners really need some level of awakening to the wreckage that they leave the home in. Here is what Tash found:

Infidelity...The Marriage Stealer

Tashika Witter Francis

The hallmark of infidelity is not necessarily sex, but secrecy. Infidelity seems best defined as a betrayal of the couple's agreement about sexual involvement and romantic entanglement outside the marriage. Infidelity may involve activity, connections, attractions or even looking at pictures or typing messages to people on the Internet. Because infidelity involves boundary setting, a couple's idiosyncratic boundaries may be influenced by families of origin, peers, culture, and gender expectations. The boundaries are not always clear (Wager, 2003). Infidelity has earned its place as a marriage stealer internationally. The reasons for infidelity in Jamaica vary. Nonetheless, "it has become such a norm in Jamaica for men to have more than one sex partner. The music and culture influence it a lot as well. The lyrics in music tell men to have more than one woman and they will be seen as someone who young boys should look up to. Some men just don't want to settle down because they just want sex" (Williams, 2014). Additionally, according to Little-White (2006), "It is said that husbands have a roving eye for attractive women." It is implied therefore that despite having a wife who may also be attractive; men are still on the lookout for more attractive women. These quotes in no way exclude women from the infidelity chain which is now becoming a prominent practice by this gender.

Research done in January 2014, *Infidelity in Jamaica: Exploring the emotional responses and coping strategies of the faithful partner*, revealed that remaining faithful in a relationship requires serious efforts on the part of both partners (Powell, 2013). The results from the phenomenological study involving seven participants (both males and females) between the ages of 20-50 years—two of whom were divorced—are clear. The emotional responses of the faithful partners facing infidelity vary; however both males and females reported feeling psychological and physical pain. Participants noted that they were depressed, hurt, ashamed, disgusted, furious and fearful after learning of their partner's unfaithfulness. They also highlighted physical symptoms of hair loss, joint pain, walking with crutches because of painful legs, inability to sleep or eat, high blood pressure and extreme loneliness. These emotional and psychosomatic responses were not unique to any one participant as many attested to similar symptoms among males and females. The research brought to the fore how damaging infidelity can be on the partner experiencing it but also on the family as a whole as it tends to lead to separation or divorce when not resolved.

Despite the pain experienced and the length of time taken to recover (if ever), having discovered their partner's infidelity; participants shared strategies used to cope during the hard times in an attempt to maintain their sanity. The coping strategies included three primary activities: (1) reading literature, (2) seeking help from friends and family members, and (3) reliance on a spiritual being. Additionally, couples sought counseling from professionals to assist in saving their relationship. This was helpful for some of the participants. A common theme for all participants, as they faced the

> *It is even more important for couples to continue to fall in love with each other every day and extend forgiveness for wrongs done in the marriage.*

infidelity monster, was prayer and frequent Bible study. Participants noted that this pulled them much closer to God and gave them strength even when they thought of ending their lives during this shameful experience.

The fact is, infidelity can be avoided in marriage relationships and should not be encouraged, owing to its deleterious effects on the family as a whole. Couples should continue therapy during marriage to help strengthen their relationship. It is even more important for couples to continue to fall in love with each other every day and extend forgiveness for wrongs done in the marriage. There are many steps that can be taken to 'infidelity–proof' marriages, but both partners must be willing to make the sacrifice. Truth is, much of what partners walk away from is waiting for them in the other relationship, especially when their motives are selfish.[11]

The personification of love is evident in Christ's grace. It is also personified in the conception of another life. Satan despises love. He detests peace and unity with Christ. Marriage represents these powerful pillars in a Christian's life. Whatever God instructs us to do, Satan tries to destroy. God and Satan are of opposing minds. God *is* love, which means Satan is everything that opposes love. If it were not for God's mercy and the influence of the Holy Spirit, adultery would be a sure way of separation and dissolving a marriage union.

Chris is still the love of my life and I am his. God never makes mistakes and He will deliver both of us if we let Him. The Bible says God hates divorce. Instead, He encourages forgiveness and constant communion with Him. Life is marred. It hurls many raw challenges and no one is perfect. Mistakes happen, but when one mistake is not effectively controlled, it then becomes the beginning of a destructive habit.

---

[11] Tashika Witter Francis, BA, MSc. authored a research paper titled *Infidelity in Jamaica: Exploring the Emotional Responses and Coping Strategies of the Faithful Partner*. Correspondence on this paper should be addressed as such. Email: tashikawitter@gmail.com

ACCEPTANCE

"Commit thy way unto the Lord; trust also in him; and he shall bring it to pass" (Ps. 37:5).

This happens to be a major part of my healing. I was brought up to believe in the ideal family, home, and society. I guess it had to be so, given the fact that Heaven is where we aim to live finally. I am so distraught by the truth of my own circustances: I do not have an ideal family unit. Thinking about it bowls me over every time. *How can this be? How did this happen?*

During our second session, my psychiatrist told me that she could not understand why I was still at that place. I understood "that place" to mean shock—the ideal life, in a bubble. She then expressed that she now understood why I am being the way I am. My Christian background taught me that love isn't easily broken, that it lasts forever, and that God intended for our marital relationship to be with one person forever—You know, all that good stuff in First Corinthians 13. So when I made my choice, I made it with the belief that the decision was perfect and would be unbreakable. Well, what a shocker! It didn't take Chris three months after our wedding before he started his embarrassing online sex stories with girls on the small university campus where I worked. Chris and I knew there was a womanizing issue that needed to be handled, an issue we really thought he had overcome, until we realized that he hadn't.

In an effort to keep the unit together and strongly knit, I pushed to "weather through the storm" and "take the bad with the good." Then, to my joy and later suffering, I got pregnant and, three months and a day after she was born, our baby girl died! I was so angry, because, to add to that grief, my husband and I were going through a divorce—an ugly one too. So, I asked, *What was all that for? Why bother to wait all my life, keep myself circumspect, stay focused, be a good Christian girl, choose my partner carefully, and then end up burying one child and divorcing her father?* That is completely the opposite kind of life I expected someone with my record to have. I felt like my head would explode! Chris wasn't even at the funeral. *What a pick, Trudean!* I was in a mess.

My psychiatrist asked me what my expectations of my soon-to-be ex-husband were and I said, "To miss me, to send money to finance his son's needs, to ask how I am coping with the death."

She said, "Why? Why do you want him to miss you?"

I said, "Because I want to know that he at least cares or cared. I want him to show something." Most times, I have felt like Chris ignored me and treated me as second-rate. Then I explained further that I have always believed that once you truly love someone, you cannot un-love that person. Jesus doesn't do that. Romans 13:10 says, "Love worketh no ill to his neighbour: therefore love is the fulfilling of the law."

So, in my mind, when my husband said "I love you," I was assured that it would be followed by his doing everything I learnt a man *should* do. My psychiatrist responded in a very insightful way that got me to pause and look at one angle that never crossed my thoughts through all this. She explained that if Chris doesn't ask me how I am or if he doesn't show actions of caring it doesn't mean he actually doesn't care. I was interpreting any indication of his lack of affection toward me to mean that he *never* really loved me, which isn't necessarily true. She explained that whatever caused him to begin acting how he did in the first place, could very well be causing him to display harsh attitudes towards me instead of showing caring. She continued by saying that it is not a reflection of me but of him.

I began to feel good that I'm paying for something I could use. *This works!* I thought silently. I began to see wisdom in her admonition. I was invalidating our past experiences within the marriage because of his actions towards me at present, not realizing the "shades of gray" that exist. Because he is being nasty now doesn't mean that he doesn't love me or has never loved me. This, my friends, was causing me the greatest pain in our relationship.

"And we have known and believed the love that God hath to us. God is love; and he that dwelleth in love dwelleth in God, and God in him" (1 John 4:16). You see, I could not understand that someone could use the word "love" and then behave the way he did. It was unfathomable to me. But, I got in check! The reality is that this is how people do. The world is full of sin and nothing except Christ can change the heart of a man or woman to transform their heart toward His love. Even then, it is difficult to get it right always. Only Jesus offers pure and transcending love. "Now our Lord Jesus Christ himself, and God, even our Father, which hath loved us, and hath given us everlasting consolation and good hope through grace, Comfort your hearts, and stablish you in every good word and work" (2 Thess. 2:16, 17).

> *So, in my mind, when my husband said "I love you," I was assured that it would be followed by his doing everything I learnt a man should do.*

My assignment this week is to begin to mourn and to face a few emotions that I had carefully tucked away, thoughts and feelings I had never gotten a chance to deal with. Along with crying, being angry and showing it, stomping a few things, ripping up Chris's pictures, laughing, and exercising, I am to face one truth and that is, there is no more Chris and Trudean. There is no more Elianah. I do not have an ideal family unit anymore. Even as I write this, my heart hurts. I was so stumped. How could my world have changed to be so absolutely, frightfully, harshly wrong?

At first, I could not write or speak in the past tense, but as I began to live against my silent wishes, I realized that hope is the attraction to a light that only the knowledge and the belief in God spark. This makes the witnessing mission more meaningful to me now. I have a better understanding of the word "saving." The world needs saving, not the red cape flying and trumpets blaring. It needs a saving of hearts. Everything happens here, which is why God wants the hearts of us all. "…The beloved of the LORD shall dwell in safety by him; and the LORD shall cover him all the day long, and he shall dwell between his shoulders" (Deut. 33:12).

> *I was so stumped. How could my world have changed to be so absolutely, frightfully, harshly wrong?*

In order to begin the healing process, I had to accept that certain aspects of my life are no more. Though it drives me into an internal sphere that cannot be described, I have also accepted that God has a perfect plan and though this stings and shatters with unforgettable reverberations, the best is yet to come. "For the LORD God is a sun and shield: the LORD will give grace and glory: no good thing will he withhold from them that walk uprightly" (Ps. 84:11). Tears fill my eyes even now. They well up not from despair, but from a promise made to me by God, and I believe it—nothing sooths me more. As a matter of fact, no one could ever excel in such a job. "And we have known and believed the love that God hath to us. God is love; and he that dwelleth in love dwelleth in God, and God in him" (1 John 4:16).

Life and death are in God's hands. I am learning a new kind of dependence, a higher and deeper level of trust. Accepting the loss of a baby and a divorce in the same year was meant to be relieving. I am trusting fully in the never-changing heart of the One who made me and brought me through this life with circumspection.

"This sickness is not unto death, but for the glory of God, that the Son of God might be glorified thereby" (John 11:4). Jesus heard the news of Lazarus' illness and death, which was believed to be imminent, yet Jesus delayed His visit. The point of this was, as He had earlier established, that this sad event was allowed by Heaven for the sake of glorifying God. Imagine if every time we asked for a miracle and it was granted how our attitude toward God would be. We would take Him for granted, and He would cease to be God and become our servant. Part of my process of acceptance was to understand that Christ performs miracles *only* for the glorification of God. Also, I had to come to terms with understanding that my request to raise Elianah was not one of those, at least not in the way I viewed it. However, one way or another, His name will ultimately be glorified, and for me, God's way is quite okay.

I am grateful for the portions of love I experienced from both Chris and Elianah. I was most happy in those times and though it is not continuous, it was good while it lasted. Greatness comes to those who have borne trials and used them to mount themselves up as they held on to Christ. He has never left me—not for a moment—and to Him I am eternally grateful and pledge my undying devotion. Jesus says, "Peace I leave with you, my peace I give unto you: not as the world giveth, give I unto you. Let not your heart be troubled, neither let it be afraid" (John 14:27).

COMFORT

*"For the LORD will not cast off for ever: But though he cause grief,
yet will he have compassion according to the multitude of his mercies.
For he doth not afflict willingly nor grieve the children of men"
(Lam. 3:31-33).*

Death struck my family closer than we could have imagined. Who knew grief would overwhelm us in such an almost paralyzing way? I still battle that numb feeling. Comfort was far away, it seemed. For days, I walked around clutching and smelling the clothes she wore that day and the blankets she died on. I wore her clip in my hair or on my clothes every day for a few weeks—sometimes, I still do.

Longing for earthly comfort—especially in times of sudden grief— is almost hopeless. But oh, how necessary it is for our survival. During all of this, I learnt that one thing is sure—calling on God for rescue will bring about peace. Such peace will come in different ways at different times, because we still tend to fight God's calm, believing that we should be constantly overwhelmed with gloom and doom. Not so! As real as pain is, so is life after death.

There are a few experiences and thoughts which made my mournful journey easier to walk, that I would like you to consider. These valuable things are still critical to my healing process as I try to move forward and upward.

Family support has value.

God expects us to be there for our family members in beautiful as well as harsh times. A supportive family is a much needed crutch that can help the wounded members walk again in a new life.

The church family's support has value.

The Bible says, "Bear ye one another's burdens, and so fulfil the law of Christ" (Gal. 6:2). What joy it was for us to have the church body wrap their love around us as we quivered under tremendous sadness and other overpowering emotions! Such a blessing! We were blessed with so many calls, prayers, visits and worship sessions. The prayers of the saints are powerful to lift any suffering soul up to Heaven for deliverance.

True friends' support has value.

"A friend loveth at all times…" (Prov. 17:17). It is comforting to have a beloved friend hold you as you melt away or cry out in deep anguish. "Comfort ye, comfort ye my people, saith your God" (Isa. 40:1).

Having someone who loves and understands you, and who *chooses* to be by your side at all stages is a most precious gift. Never be taken for granted, it is a silent ministry and a powerful medicine for broken people.

Belief in God and His Word is the most important.

"Jesus said unto her, I am the resurrection and the life: he that believeth in me, though he were dead, yet shall he live" (John 11:25). "Blessed and holy is he that hath part in the first resurrection: on such the second death hath no power, but they shall be priests of God and of Christ, and shall reign with him a thousand years" (Rev. 20:6). These powerful texts give me great strength in moving on and looking up. I am now challenged to live a life that counts so that I can benefit from this hope of life with Christ after an earthly death. I have an appointment with my baby girl that I *must* keep when Jesus comes. I cannot imagine how I would cope with losing her if there was no hope after this life! The assurance in Isaiah 41:10 is calming as well as sobering. It says, "Fear thou not, for I am with thee: be not dismayed; for I am thy God: I will strengthen thee; yea, I will help thee; yea I will uphold thee with the right hand of my righteousness."

The truth is that it could have been worse.

Fortunately for us Christians, we believe, "The LORD upholdeth all that fall, and raiseth up all those that be bowed down" (Ps. 145:14). God never leaves His children.

Moving on seems grim. Lifting your leg to make that very first step toward what lies ahead is almost grueling. I remember thinking, "How dare the world go on!" Whether I wanted to or not, the world was spinning just the same, and I had to eat when my tummy growled, laugh when my brother told a really good joke, play when my three-year-old son wanted to be chased or tickled, do house chores, and return to work. Packing up Elianah's things and giving them away will be quite an overwhelming task, but I have to keep clinging to the bright hope that, one day, the heavens will roll open and Jesus will be there, ready to put my precious little baby girl in my arms once again. The text that kept replaying in my head at Elianah's Celebration Service was Revelation 21:4: "And God shall wipe away all tears from their eyes; and there shall be no more death, neither sorrow, nor crying, neither shall there be any more pain: for the former things are passed away." Isn't that beautiful?

Here are life highlights to remember:

- Be always grateful, honest, loving and kind.
- Keep healthy and keep on praising the Lord.
- Stay connected to God through prayer.
- Get wisdom from His word, and embrace the truth—it will make you free.[12]

It is vital that to remember Philippians 4:13, "[We] can do all things through Christ who strengtheneth [us]." In Mark 9:23, Jesus says, "If thou canst believe, all things are possible to him that believeth."

In a kind effort to comfort me, people send me notes to remind me that I am being prayed for. One of my friends Tony W. (author of "*The Courage to Conquer*"), sent this note to me:

> Already, your young life has been fraught with pain and trouble. Your marriage crumbled. Your last child died. You had to leave…and relocate to another country. Some people lose their faith in Christ due to deep trial and unanswered questions. Others grow in strength under adversity. God never promised us a life free from pain, temptation and adversity, and I am convinced that the more we seek to serve Him, the more Satan challenges us. Check the following account of the great apostle Paul:
>
> "Are they ministers of Christ? (I speak as a fool) I am more; in labours more abundant, in stripes above measure, in prisons more frequent, in deaths oft. Of the Jews five times received I forty stripes save one. Thrice was I beaten with rods, once was I stoned, thrice I suffered shipwreck, a night and a day I have been in the deep; In journeyings often, in perils of waters, in perils of robbers, in perils by mine own countrymen, in perils by the heathen, in perils in the city, in perils in the wilderness, in perils in the sea, in perils among false brethren; In weariness and painfulness, in watchings often, in hunger and thirst, in fastings often, in cold and nakedness. Beside those things that are without, that which cometh upon me daily, the care of all the churches" (2 Cor. 11:23–28).
>
> So do not despair. Have faith in God. When I was young, we used to sing a hymn in church, a line of which went like this:
>
> "The bud may have a bitter taste/ But sweet will be the flower."[13]
>
> Your life is a bud. The best is yet to come as the flower blooms.

---

12 "And ye shall know the truth, and the truth shall make you free" (John 8:32).

13 This is a line from the hymn, God Moves in a Mysterious Way, written by William Cowper in 1773.

My wife Jean and I leave this magnificent blessing with you and trust that God will fulfill it in you every step of the way. Cheers!

I was quite encouraged by this thoughtful note and very moved by Paul's perilous experiences. Those of us who suffer pain are not alone—we never were. Don't get side-tracked by Satan and be led into the foolish thinking that you have been exiled or dismissed from the presence of God. Sin spares no one, but God's grace is more than abundant.

Another note that brought some level of appreciative comfort came from one of those inspirational thoughts my friend, Steve L., always sends out to us. This devotional thought was titled, "Problems & Trials":

"We can rejoice, too, when we run into problems and trials, for we know that they help us develop endurance. And endurance develops strength of character, and character strengthens our confident hope of salvation" (Rom. 5:3, 4, NLT).

[Did you know that] the way you handle adversities has a huge impact on your success in life? If you shrink back and choose to get bitter and lose your enthusiasm, then you are allowing the difficulties of life to bury you. You are allowing hardship to keep you from God's true purpose for your life. But if you choose to keep pressing forward in Jesus' name with a smile on your face, rejoicing even in the hard times, you are allowing God's character to be developed inside of you. You become a better mirror of His goodness and people can be drawn to Him because of the sermon and testimonies of His goodness that they see in your life.

Think about this: the only difference between a piece of black coal and a priceless diamond is the amount of pressure that it has endured. When you stand strong in the midst of the trials and difficulties in life, when you allow God to shape and mold your character, it's like going from a piece of coal to a priceless diamond. Those difficulties are going to give way to new growth, new potential, new talent, new friendships, new opportunities, and new vision. You're going to see your life blossom in ways that you've never even dreamed!

I have included these two notes sent me to share the blessings I have received from people around me. Some people have no such experience, and it makes the grieving process longer and less bearable. Even though Chris is not integral in my healing process as he should be, God has nudged many people to send encouraging thoughts to propel me on. I do not take them for granted, and I most certainly will continue to thank them for their acts of kindness.

Today, accept this as my thought to you, from a friend who understands and cares.

PRAISE THROUGH PAIN

"Praise ye the LORD: for it is good to sing praises unto our God; for it is pleasant; and praise is comely" (Ps. 147:1).

Writing this book about my story was very difficult because it caused me to slowly relive details I would have rather forgotten. But I was impressed by the Holy Spirit to share my experience so that someone else can meet God or remember Him as they go through their own trying time. God has been amazing, sheltering, and the Only One to bring me peace. It has simply been an awesome experience!

Please take the time to let God's Words penetrate through your being while you daily reflect on His truly amazing mercy and powers. His Words are life and they are true. They rescued me and they can rescue you. A few of the many supporting biblical texts for grieving, suffering, or hurt souls are listed below. My friends and family insisted that I be reminded of Christ's Words to me. Now I am sharing them with you. I am quite sure they can help you too. They definitely made me stronger.

Courage and Strength
- "Behold, God is my salvation; I will trust, and not be afraid: for the LORD JEHOVAH is my strength and my song; he also is become my salvation" (Isa. 12:2).
- "What shall we then say to these things? If God be for us, who can be against us?" (Rom. 8:31).
- "Be strong and of a good courage, fear not, nor be afraid of them: for the LORD thy God, he it is that doth go with thee. he will not fail thee nor forsake thee. And Moses called unto Joshua and said unto him in the sight of all Israel, 'Be strong and of a good courage: for thou must go with this people unto the land which the Lord hath sworn unto their fathers to give them; and thou shalt cause them to inherit it. And the Lord, he it is that doth go before thee; he will be with thee, he will not fail thee; neither forsake thee: fear not, neither be dismayed" (Deut. 31:6–8).

- "He giveth power to the faint; and to them that have no might he increaseth strength. Even the youths shall faint and be weary, and the young men shall utterly fall: But they that wait upon the LORD shall renew their strength; they shall mount up with wings as eagles; they shall run, and not be weary; and they shall walk, and not faint" (Isa. 40: 29–31).
- "But now, thus saith the LORD, that created thee, O Jacob, and he that formed thee, O Israel, Fear not: for I have redeemed thee, I have called thee by thy name; thou art mine. When thou passest through the waters, I will be with thee; and through the rivers, they shall not overflow thee: when thou walkest through the fire, thou shalt not be burned; neither shall the flame kindle thee" (Isa. 43:1–2).
- "The Lord will give strength unto his people; the LORD will bless His people with peace" (Ps. 29:11).
- "My soul followeth hard after thee: thy right hand upholdeth me" (Ps. 63:8).
- "Thou hast a mighty arm: strong is thy hand, and high is thy right hand. Justice and judgment are the habitation of thy throne: mercy and truth shall go before thy face" (Ps. 89:13–14).
- "Ye shall not need to fight in this battle: set yourselves, stand ye still, and see the salvation of the Lord, with you, O Judah and Jerusalem: fear not, nor be dismayed; to morrow go out against them: for the LORD will be with you" (2 Chron. 20:17).

Life and Death
- "But is now made manifest by the appearing of our Saviour Jesus Christ, who hath abolished death, and hath brought life and immortality to light through the gospel:" (2 Tim. 1:10).
- "Precious in the sight of the LORD is the death of his saints" (Ps. 116:15).
- "But God will redeem my soul from the power of the grave: for he shall receive me" (Ps. 49:15).
- "But if the Spirit of him that raised up Jesus from the dead dwell in you, he that raised up Christ from the dead shall also quicken your mortal bodies by his Spirit that dwelleth in you" (Rom. 8:11).
- "Jesus said unto her, I am the resurrection and the life: he who believeth in Me, though he were dead, yet shall he live. And whosoever liveth and believeth in me shall never die. Believest thou this?" (John 11:25–26).
- "And God shall wipe away all tears from their eyes; and there shall be no more death, neither sorrow, nor crying, neither shall there be any more pain: for the former things are passed away" (Rev. 21:4).
- "And many of them that sleep in the dust of the earth shall awake, some to everlasting life, and some to shame and everlasting contempt" (Dan. 12:2).

Peace
- "Peace I leave with you, my peace I give unto you: not as the world giveth, give I unto you. Let not your heart be troubled, neither let it be afraid" (John 14:27).
- "And let the peace of God rule in your hearts, to the which also ye are called in one body; and be ye thankful" (Col. 3:15).
- "Mark the perfect man, and behold the upright: for the end of that man is peace" (Ps. 37:37).

Faith
- "Watch ye, stand fast in the faith, quit you like men, be strong" (1 Cor. 16:13).
- "For by grace are ye saved through faith; and that not of yourselves: it is the gift of God" (Eph. 2:8).
- "And Jesus answering saith unto them, Have faith in God. For verily I say unto you, That whosoever shall say unto this mountain, Be thou removed, and be thou cast into the sea; and shall not doubt in his heart, but shall believe that those things which he saith shall come to pass; he shall have whatsoever he saith. Therefore I say unto you, What things soever ye desire, when ye pray, believe that ye receive them, and ye shall have them" (Mark 11:22–24).

Trust
- "God is our refuge and strength, a very present help in trouble.
- Therefore will not we fear, though the earth be removed
- and though the mountains be carried into the midst of the sea" (Ps. 46:1–2).
- "Fear not, little flock; for it is your Father's good pleasure to give you the kingdom" (Luke 12:32).
- "Wait on the LORD: be of good courage, and he shall strengthen thine heart: wait, I say, on the LORD" (Ps. 27:14).
- "The LORD is good, a strong hold in the day of trouble; and he knoweth them that trust in Him" (Nah. 1:7).

Praise Him! Your glass is half full.

EXTRAORDINARY MOMENTS WITH GOD

"Draw nigh to God, and he will draw nigh to you. Cleanse your hands, ye sinners; and purify your hearts, ye double minded"
(James 4:8).

This chapter is written with memories of impressive encounters with God that readers may be firmly encouraged through my experience. When we are sure that God is with us and He cares, it helps direct us. Personally, these specially chosen experiences reiterate why I choose moment by moment to believe and listen to Him. One in particular occurred prior to this year's grieving experiences and, therefore, has pulled my mind back to times when God came through for me. The moments remind me that Christ is very present[14] and wants us to fall back on Him in order to be carried.

1

"For the prophecy came not in old time by the will of man: but holy men of God spake as they were moved by the Holy Ghost"
(2 Peter 1:21).

One day—a very normal work day—I walked into the university café to buy something to eat. As I paid for my meal, the cashier charmingly got my attention. We were used to exchanging courteous and polite chit-chat. A very pleasant lady, she said that she had been impressed to pray with me, she did—right then. When he finished and had continued cashing, she explained why she had just prayed with me.

---

14 "God is our refuge and strength, a very present help in trouble" (Ps. 46:1).

To my surprise, she said that God told her to pray for me right then, and she would not have been comfortable letting me leave without doing so. She said, "No weapon formed against you shall prosper."[15] She continued to complete our transaction. "You are very private. I don't need to know what is going on, but God says everything will be okay." As I stood in silence and awe, she continued, "Oh, and He said to tell you that He is working on that relationship." She squeezed my outstretched arm and smiled assuredly.

By this time, tears were welling up in my eyes, but I could not afford to spill them there. So, I tried to leave before anyone saw what was really happening. I'm not sure why I did that, but it is probably because I am so used to controlling how I feel that letting go or releasing my emotions is very hard. I thanked her with all my heart and left. I am sure she saw all over my face and posture the effect of her prayer and words.

When I got back to the office, I shared my experience with my boss, and later, with my girlfriend. Of course, they received my report with a bit of skepticism because they weren't sure who she was and, more importantly, because it seemed that the relationship message pointed to Chris.

That prayer and message from God had stunned me into deep silence. I have always heard of individuals who received such revelations coming from utter strangers and I have wondered how authentic it was. Here is the thing though: I *did* pray to God a very long time ago to make His will known to me by using a neutral person or complete stranger. I wanted no bias perspective, for I hadn't trusted myself to be sure of what God was saying to me. One thing is certain, as I write to you now, the pages of my life, in real time, are continuously turning and being written upon. I am longing, as are all my friends and family, to see what is at the chapter's end.

> *Just as I felt like my insides were about to cave in, the gentlest voice I have ever heard said to me, "I am going to take her."*

2

"And when the Lord saw her, he had compassion on her, and said unto her, Weep not" (Luke 7:13).

This flashback of an experience is also profound. I knew that it was the soothing voice of God. As I stood by Elianah's bedside, trying to sing "Jesus Loves the Little Children," my voice began to crack as I saw death creeping over her. Just as I felt like my insides were about to cave in, the gentlest voice I have ever heard said to me, "I am going to take her."

---

15 "No weapon that is formed against thee shall prosper; and every tongue that shall rise against thee in judgment thou shalt condemn. This is the heritage of the servants of the LORD, and their righteousness is of me, saith the LORD" (Isa. 54:17).

I felt like falling and being defiant, but for some unexplainable reason, I also felt that it would be okay and that He could go ahead and have her. Yet, it hurt. It was then that I accepted that I would not be taking her home. I told this to no one, even as people around me tried to boost their faith and mine and even as they sent off requests to Heaven for a miraculous working.

"When Jesus therefore saw her weeping, and the Jews also weeping which came with her, he groaned in the spirit, and was troubled" (John 11:33).

I do not believe that Jesus is insensitive, slack in His use of His Might, or harsh in His judgment. I know that He felt my pain that awful day, and I believe Heaven cried with me, but not with a thought of finality. Jesus carries me now. I live this. Sin is real and isn't something to dabble in or request a pass to escape. Sin has no mercy. It spares no one, and we suffer from it in one form or another. Christ is the doorway out. He lives to prove that bliss is yet to come, and He is personally handling that bliss for each of His children.

3

"Casting all your care upon him; for he careth for you" (1 Peter 5:7).

There are little things and perfect timing of miracles that remind me that God is alive and is involved in our affairs. He cares so much that great and small details are of equal importance. Our happiness is all He wants us to have. I needed some money to complete a transaction, and I didn't have enough for the transaction and the remaining bills for the month. This hadn't happened in a few months, but that is what happens when illness is a constant recurring issue. I told my brother about it, but ended the conversation saying, "God will handle it." I was thoroughly convinced that there was no need to worry. In fact, worrying wouldn't get me the money I wanted; if anything, it might *cause* me to spend money for medication. My stress was at a dangerous level and I would have no more of it!

I was to attend an informal dinner with a few friends from Jamaica, but they were delayed so I ate at home with the intention of not attending. Fortunately, they came for me. I was abole to go and enjoy some food with them. Upon my leaving, one of my more mature friends slipped something into my hand. I tried resisting, but it was done so privately that any refusals would have embarrassed us both. He said, "Use it for Michael." That was a trick to get me to keep it, I figured. I didn't try to count it right then, though I knew it was money. When I got home, I told my brother and unfolded the money. It was enough to complete my transaction, take care of our needs for the rest of the month, and extend help to a friend who was also tapped out. We praised God for the entire week. He is awesome, and no one can compare to His matchless grace. Wouldn't you agree?

"[A]nd pray one for another, that ye may be healed. The effectual fervent prayer of a righteous man availeth much" (James 5:16).

One night Elianah had terrible gripping discomfort. No one could sleep. I had just come from the pharmacy where I had gotten medication for my pain when my girlfriend, Tashika, came over to relate how the evening was going for her. I was so tired and miserable; I could not move very fast and I really needed sleep. Tashika, said to my son, "Michael, why don't you pray and ask God to make Elianah feel better." Like the child God wants us to be, Michael obediently knelt down beside his sister and prayed for her to feel better. Almost instantly, Elianah stopped crying and soon went to sleep. We were all amazed, not in disbelief, but because we had witnessed, first–hand another act of God. God is truly with us.

"But I trusted in thee, O LORD: I said, Thou art my God" (Ps. 31:14).

Looking for a place to live is exhausting. Finding the place that suits you and your family's needs is all the more daunting. My mother said, "God knows where it is, just don't worry."

I said, "I know He knows where it is. I just want Him to show *me* where it is. He knows what I want and He will give it to me for the price I can afford." Without any form of exaggeration, I am telling you this: the next day I found it. After searching for a few weeks, it was right there. I am writing to you from that very place today. It had been sitting here for me to see, but because the realtor and I could not get a compatible timetable, I never saw it until I had handed the matter over to God. It is perfect for my family. I praise God for dwelling among us in spite of our doubts and faulty habits. Christ deserves our worship!

"And this is the confidence that we have in him, that, if we ask any thing according to his will, he heareth us:" (1 John 5:14).

In 2005, I went to Trinidad and Tobago to complete a master's degree in educational psychology through an Andrews University affiliated program there. I had never visited the country before and only knew two people there at the time. I had gone there without sufficient means to pay my tuition. The only money I had was from a very good friend of mine who was impressed with my move and gave me money to pay for my first class. That was just more ammunition for me to push on through. Frankly, I felt called to go and I did so against all the advice of my family members. For them, it was about seeing my way there, having a working plan, and being sure of its results. For me, it was about the faith I needed to exercise and the peace I felt. Chris was in support of my going even though his heart was sad. I loved him even more for encouraging me to pursue a higher goal.

When I touched my feet to the ground at the Piarco International Airport in Trinidad, I remember feeling dizzy and all warm inside. The only time I had done anything like this was for a mission trip in Mexico, but, in going there, I had been quite sure that it was God's work I was doing. This situation was a whole new world.

A few days after arriving, I paced outside my friend's office sometime after five o'clock when it was all clear. I was concerned about affording my tuition and my livelihood. I remember distinctly what I said to God in that corridor. I said, "God, You brought me here and since You brought me here, You need to find a job for me to take care of myself. I'm not leaving this corridor until I get one!" I was serious. So I continued pacing.

Then He said to me, almost with a laugh in His voice, "Trudean, go home." At first I was hesitant because I had just said that I was not going to leave the hallway until I got a job. Yet, I complied.

When I got to the house, I remembered what God had just told me and went on in. As I pushed the front door open, my friend and another gentleman were chatting at the table by the door. Then, as unbelievable as it may sound, the gentleman whom I had never seem before said to me, "Would you like to work for us?" I had to find a seat immediately. I wanted to scream, cry, pray, laugh, and just stare. Just like that, it had happened. The rest is history: I worked there for five years, got married to Chris when he moved there, had my first child there, and graduated with a degree and all bills paid. I say, "Nothing but God."

DECISIONS, DECISIONS, DECISIONS

"Trust in the LORD with all thine heart and lean not unto thine own understanding. In all thy ways acknowledge him, and he shall direct thy paths" (Prov. 3:5, 6).

This chapter is designed to help you make some manageably small yet progressive steps. To get to this point in my life, I had to make numerous decisions concerning my life and how I was to move on. I simply had to make these decisions for they were coming at me even when I wasn't ready to make them. So, instead of trying to evade them, I resolutely decided to confront them. We have to make all sorts of decisions each day, some are inconsequential and some are life-changing; They range from what color blouse or tie we will wear to how many children we'd like to have and with whom. We decide many things like who we will call friends, what we will eat, what time we will sleep, which route we will take to get to work, and what time we will arrive. The fact that we must make decisions is inescapable. So what are you going to do about it?

One night, during my time of regular introspection, I asked myself to describe the pain I felt. This was possibly by virtue of the consistent requests made by my therapists to perform this internal activity. When I could put my finger on it, this is what I wrote: "Sometimes the pain makes me feel like my body is disintegrating into a million irreplaceable and untraceable pieces. It's like fragments of me are floating away bit by bit into my imagination. I have to grab at the ones I can see leaving me and find a place—some place to fit them into. God knows that I know He is there, but He also knows and understands that I was and still am in pain." This isn't a strange thought. Even God knows this

> *The difference between Christians and the rest of the world is that we feel pain because of the natural emotions circumstances bring, but when it comes to death, the pain we feel is not void of hopefulness.*

very feeling. I believe there was pain in the heart of God even though He knew His Son would be alive again in just three days.

The difference between Christians and the rest of the world is that *we* feel pain because of the natural emotions circumstances bring, but when it comes to death, the pain we feel is not void of hopefulness. Though we cry, we know that the greatest miraculous experiences are ahead. This gleam of hope makes our feelings of pain fade away or simply easier to bear.

There are three things I had to decide to do—control stress, forgive, and accept.

Control stress. I had to decide to control my stress levels. You see there are three prongs to be mindful of where this "silent killer"[16] is concerned: the *internal and external causes*, the *actual stimuli*, and the *reaction to stress*. Stressful situations will come no matter how smart you are at dodging them. This is not easy. Humans are stress magnets. Sometimes we seem to *like* being stressed out to the point of fraying. This is mainly because we share a world with other people who are different from us and we cannot control anything or anyone except ourselves and what we do. How we treat the events in our lives will determine the success of our outcomes.

Moderate amounts of stress are good, but my stress was fast approaching the life threatening level. I got help. Even though I was monitoring myself, my psychiatrists and psychologist were very helpful in monitoring my stress levels as well. First, I had to begin to identify the triggers—"fight-or-flight." Second, I had to find ways to avoid these triggers. Third, I had to control my reactions to stressful experiences, which is the last part and the most challenging.

In his book, "*Mental and Emotional Health*," Dr. Julián Melgosa gave spiritual insights for coping with stress. Many of God's people and even Jesus Himself met stressful situations and had to find meaningful and beneficial ways of handling them.

- Jesus kept close to His Father. He relied on Him for His daily doses of strength and wisdom. He was fully aware of life's challenges, and He knew that He needed Heaven's help to handle it all.
- Jesus fellowshipped with others; recreation is important, especially when it's among God's natural creations. Godly friends are very helpful in stressful times too.
- Jesus helped others. Engage yourself in meaningful work. Jesus's life was filled with support for others in need. What a great pattern to follow! It is true that helping others does make you feel better. There is something healing about selfless actions. Try it.
- Jesus also engaged in exercise. Walk. Keeping both your body and mind fit through exercise and a meaningful prayer life will make you more resilient. Don't sit around feeling sorry for yourself and become secluded. Practicing these two

---

16 Cohen, Martin V. "Stress: The Silent Killer." MartinVCohen.com. 2000. http://www.martinvcohen.com/stress.html. (Accessed November 4, 2015).

things make the mind and body more in sync, thereby enabling a more productive attitude and effective decision making.

Q: What kinds of stress do you want God to handle for you? Take a few moments to jot them down.
1. _____
2. _____
3. _____

Forgive. Ephesians 4:32 says, "And be ye kind one to another, tenderhearted, forgiving one another even as God for Christ's sake hath forgiven you." My students are usually amazed at the positive correlation between having a forgiving attitude and a healthy body. The discussions are usually moving. An unforgiving spirit doesn't hurt the perpetrator of all your ills, it hurts *you*. Forgiving others begins the healing process. I had decided to forgive myself for feeling guilty about our daughter's death. I had to *decide* to forgive my husband for not being with me while she died, during the funeral preparations, and at the funeral. I thought I had done so until Pastor Telemaque[17] prayed with me and admonished me to reach in and forgive him. I couldn't see why he thought I hadn't. I guessed that it came over to him through our communication that my forgiveness for Chris was still incomplete. I read the texts he sent me, prayed the kinds of prayers he suggested, and then—what a surprise!—I was still angry and deeply wounded.

When I confronted my true thoughts on it all, I told Chris how I felt about everything over the years and I began to feel better. Then, to my disbelief, I was once again, falling in love with my husband all over again. I began to see the spiritual battle and our human frailties as well as Christ's exemplary love for us. (Naturally, this new development must be left for my next book.) I decided to keep forgiving because I want to be forgiven. John 15:12, 14 shares God's wish for relationships: "This is my commandment, That ye love one another, as I have loved you...Ye are my friends, if ye do whatsoever I command you."

Q: Who do you need to forgive and for what?
1. Name: _____ Infraction:_____
2. Name: _____ Infraction:_____
3. Name: _____ Infraction:_____

Accept: When I analyzed my decisions and how to share them in item form, it dawned on me that they all are linked to one thing—trust in God. I had decided to move by

---

[17] More information about Pastor Samuel Telemaque can be found on the following websites:
"Pastor Samuel Telemaque." ZoomInfo.com. http://www.zoominfo.com/p/Samuel-Telemaque/164862245. (Accessed November 5, 2015).
"Senate President challenges Adventists." Jamaica Observer. 27 Jan. 2014. http://www.jamaicaobserver.com/news/Senate-President-challenges-Adventists_15866678. (Accessed November 5, 2015).

lessening my stress level and improving my reactions toward them. In essence, that means, I decided to trust God more. "Commit thy way unto the LORD; trust also in him; and he shall bring it to pass" (Ps. 37:5). Amazing peace! Trusting in God meant I had to say yes to His will, which included His withholding His hand from saving my daughter from death. Practically speaking, *trusting God* also meant I had to do the following:

- accept my losses, past and present
- accept who and what I do have
- accept that I am overly stressed and depressed and in need of help
- accept that God controls it all both by will and permission
- accept that sin touches everyone and none can escape it

Then I had to decide to *control me* in a more effective manner by doing the following:

- avoiding stressful situations
- taking my life in simple strides
- depending more on God
- staying in touch with Heaven
- reassuring myself that God's Word is truth

Being in a stressful state can prevent us from hearing the Holy Spirit and from understanding God's present Will for our lives. The devil is an imp, and his wiles are quite clever. When we accept a state of defeat, we are telling God that He has no power over the situation and that the battle is already lost. It is here that our greatest enemy lurks and feeds our minds on unhealthy and debasing thoughts.

It is only by deciding to live a life devoted to God that we can truly experience a significant reduction in stress and a powerful growth in how we manage it. There will be challenges, especially for children of God, but acknowledging that God is near makes a world of difference. There will be nothing but joy amidst it all—nothing but joy! "These things have I spoken unto you, that my joy might remain in you, and that your joy might be full" (John 15:11).

Q: What things do you need to accept in order to move on?
1. _____
2. _____
3. _____
4. _____
5. _____

Give Jesus all that rests on your heart. Believing in His Word and living His will should be evident in our lives when things come to disturb our waters. We should experience less anxiety, less frustration, and less fear.

Be resilient. Start over. Move on. Whichever of these suits you best, use it. Life is going to happen. You will automatically try to survive your pain; it is part of our coping mechanisms. We are not in control of our lives as much as we'd like to be. Some people choose to take their lives, but, in the end, life will be restored and an answer will have to be given before the final act of judgment. We have no control there. The thing we do control is our choice to "bat well." We cannot control the pitcher or the ball, just how we swing when it has been thrown our way.

There are five stages of grieving that I learnt about in school: *denial, anger, bargaining, depression and acceptance*[18] (See Kubler Ross' model for more details, pg 71). These phases or stages of grieving have no time limit and should not be rushed. Sometimes you may encounter tactless comments from individuals trying to help you "pick yourself up," but nonetheless, set your own goal and be patient with yourself. You can do it. If you couldn't, then God would be wrong, for the first time! Thankfully, He *cannot* be wrong.

Psalm 91:12 is a firm reminder that you will not be trekking alone if you decide to set out on the healing journey; angels will help: "They shall bear thee up in their hands, lest thou dash thy foot against a stone." Be open to the help Heaven sends your way. Your mental abilities are stronger than you give yourself credit for and you should trust God with it, for He has promised that He will never leave us or forsake us. (Heb. 13:5).

If we want to live a healthy life, which includes moving on from a lower state to a higher one, then we have to comply with Jesus' high recommendation. Even in this marred world, it works! "Abide in me, and I in you. As the branch cannot bear fruit of itself, except it abide in the vine; no more can ye, except ye abide in me. I am the vine, ye are the branches: He that abideth in me, and I in him, the same bringeth forth much fruit: for without me ye can do nothing. If a man abide not in me, he is cast forth as a branch, and is withered; and men gather them, and cast them into the fire, and they are burned. If ye abide in me, and my words abide in you, ye shall ask what ye will, and it shall be done unto you" (John 15:4—7). Isn't this one guarantee you'd *like* to cash in on?

---

18 See Table 1- *The Grieving Process*, as understood from Elisabeth Kübler-Ross' model and illustrated by *Lasting Solutions*.

Table 1. The Grieving Process

Grieving Process	What you're feeling	What you may need
Denial	• Shock • Numbness • Anxiety	• Time to Absorb Information • Reality Check
Anger	• Fear • Like screaming • Revenge • Blaming • Frustration • Confusion • Resistance	• Safe place to vent • Support • Permission to "feel" the loss
Bargaining	• Replaying of events • Thinking you can change the outcome	• Someone to listen to you • Confirmation of the reality • Time to think things through
Depression	• Tiredness • Inability to relax • Lack of focus • Worthlessness • No way out • Darkness everywhere • Inability to move forward • Feeling immobilized	• To see a doctor or therapist • A good shoulder to cry on • Someone to guide you through • A kick in the butt • Something to focus on • Encouragement • Opportunity to explore • New Starting Point
Acceptance	• Less pain • More energy • More focus • Feel lighter • Commitment to moving forward	• Direction • Reinforcement • Acknowledgement • Adjustment and Focus

WEEP NOT

"And all wept, and bewailed her: but he said, Weep not; she is not dead, but sleepeth" (Luke 8:52).

"For as the sufferings of Christ abound in us, so our consolation also aboundeth by Christ" (2 Cor. 1:5).

When your parents say, "Don't worry," or "I will buy it for your birthday," or "I love you," don't you feel an overcoming peace? When you hear reassuring and positive words from the ones you love, isn't there relief and confidence that takes over any previous doubt? There are times when I had to leave Michael with a sitter for a few hours and with my mother for a few days or weeks. Whenever he sees me leaving him behind, his face gets into a shape that signals tears are near. However, after I hug him tightly and look him steadily in the eyes and say, "Michael, I am coming back," his countenance changes. It's always been so, since the first time I had to leave him to return to work. It was I who ended up crying. There are no attachment issues with him, for he feels secure in our relationship. Why is that?

It is because I keep my word. My son knows that if I say that I will be back in two days, on Sunday, in a few hours, tomorrow, and so on, I will be back—just as I said I would. I also keep in touch with him as often as he can tolerate, just to touch base to let him know that I love and remember him and just to fill him in on the things I am doing to prepare for my return to him. This makes his days lighter, and he can be happy without unpleasant distractions.

Now, that is my son. That is a child that I carried. Is his world perfect? Not at all. Yet, if he can do it, what is preventing grown people from doing the same? What prevents people who are considered adults with higher levels of intelligence and a greater control over choices and outcomes from experiencing secure attachment with our Father and His Son? Is it our Father's fault? Certainly not, then we would be in the right! Right? So, if Jesus says that He has gone to the Father's house prepare a mansion for us (see John 14:1–3), leaves a set of simple instructions for us to follow so that we can be safe and ready to leave with

Him when He returns, why can't we trust Him to do just that? How come He is having trouble with trusting us to do just as He asked? Ironically, the commands that He left are for our protection and lasting happiness. What seems to be the glitch? We expect our kids to do it; we even expect our parents to keep their words, so how come we expect differently of God? We mete our sanctions to our children when they act against our wishes. Are we expecting a different standard of God? "Now therefore hearken unto me, O ye children: for blessed are they that keep my ways. Hear instruction, and be wise, and refuse it not" (Prov. 8:32—33). Is it any wonder that Jesus said that we need to be like children to enter the kingdom of heaven? The Bible even says: "As newborn babes, desire the sincere milk of the word that ye may grow thereby:" (1 Peter 2:2). There is something about being childlike that we should not ignore.

Sometimes, we make a mess of things in trying to take things over. Sometimes, the more freedom we are given, the wilder we become. Sometimes, when we are treated with tenderness and genuine love, we take it for granted and run to the things that offer us mediocrity. Is this not significantly warped behavior? Is it not now clear that something or someone is blinding us or selling us a mirage of beautiful lies?

During my initial stages of grieving, I had to frantically draw for scriptural references to keep me sane. Immediately, my mind went in to overdrive to source any information from the Bible and other inspirational materials that would give the kind of hope a grieving mother would need to survive the early hours and days. When I found the scripture that spoke of how the dead in Christ will rise first and we that are alive and have remained in Christ will be caught up to meet them in the air at the sound of the first trumpet, I rested there (see 1 Thessalonians 4:16–18). Revelation 21:4 was another of my favorite texts, "And God shall wipe away all tears from their eyes; and there shall be no more death, neither sorrow, nor crying, neither shall there be any more pain: for the former things are passed away."

In one grim recounting of the death of a mother's only son, the Bible tells us that Jesus told the mother not to cry. "And when the Lord saw her, he had compassion on her, and said unto her, Weep not" (Luke 7:13). In another tragic account of a dead daughter, Jesus told the people, "Weep not; she is not dead, but sleepeth" (Luke 8:52). When Jesus was sentenced to death by crucifixion by Pilate, He told the women not to cry for Him: "[W]eep not for me, but weep for yourselves, and for your children" (Luke 23:28).

Now how can we *not* weep at the loss of our loved ones? It seems like a harsh request. In my experience, "weep not" doesn't mean that tears should not be shed (after all, Ecclesiastes 3: 4 says there is a time to weep). Rather, it means that, if you believe in Christ and His Word, you will cry but for a time and with the understanding that heaven is real and that Jesus will resurrect His own in His time. This puts a new spin on things, I'd say. If your loved ones die in sin, you can see why there should be weeping, for a soul is forever lost. However, if your loved one dies in Christ, then just as day follows night, that person will live again, but this time forever!

As a mother, the thought of seeing my sweet baby girl again in her purest of forms make me happy. I can hardly keep still because I yearn to hold and hug her tightly again.

I miss her every day, but I have a burning hope that keeps my flame lit each morning. For me, it is that simple: God says it, and I decided to believe it! I trust Him. I trust that He isn't a myth concocted to keep people in line with the laws of western lands but that His Life and death are real and that the Bible is written proof of this.

Personal experiences are important in our Christian journey. Through these first-hand encounters with Christ, we get to yield more willingly. With practice, we need less prodding. No one can live our lives for us simply because God designed it to be so. We each have our own choices to make. In this instance, we have to choose to stay with God, delve into His Word, and believe it daily. It is our lifeline. Death can swallow the living just as it did the ones we mourn over. But our "fight or flight" response system is designed to protect us from such tragedies. When we feel overwhelmed, disheartened or stressed, we should call on the name of Jesus and bow before Him. Then we will receive the power that only Heaven can give to enable us to press on.

There is an old adage I grew up hearing which goes like this: "Belief kills and belief cures." Believe that! In our case, we will say, "Believing heals." Actually, it serves my purpose better to believe God. Life makes more sense to me now. There is a clearer direction. Salvation officially makes sense! Jesus says, "He that believeth and is baptized shall be saved; but he that believeth not shall be damned" (Mark 16:16). I want to be saved, so I choose to believe, even now. Like Hannah, I am changing my countenance in anticipation of what is to come. I am changing my attitude to one that shows a faithful disposition because I know my request will be granted.

When I read the accounts of Peter walking on water[19] and of trumpets blasting and the Jericho walls falling down[20] without so much as a finger being lifted, I am awestruck and filled with wonder. Some of us even wonder if we will ever be so blessed as to witness or be recipients of such unbelievable miracles. The phenomenal thing is, as one wise person puts it, that circumstances should not control our faith. What do you think will happen when we start telling our problems that God is bigger than they are? Imagine for a minute what our life would be if these problems we have right now became insignificant or even non-existent. Our faith should not be influenced by how daunting these experiences are for us. Imagine what will change when we put our priorities in the correct ranking order?

"…Weep not: behold, the Lion of the tribe of Juda, the Root of David, hath prevailed to open the book, and to loose the seven seals thereof" (Rev. 5:5). Don't cry. You know how the story ends.

---

[19] The story of Peter walking on water can be found in Matthew 14:22—33, Mark 6:45—53, and John 6:15—21.

[20] The story of the destruction of the city of Jericho can be found in Joshua 6:1—21.

HELLO AND GOODBYE

"Therefore if any man be in Christ, he is a new creature: old things are passed away; behold, all things are become new" (2 Cor. 5:17).

I'm sitting on my bed in the corner of my room, and the atmosphere is filled with sounds of fireworks lighting up the night sky in recognition of the New Year's approach in a few hours. It is December 31, 2014 and the time is now 8:26 p.m. I'm guessing the anticipation is high, which is why I'm hearing all these fiery explosions of excitement around me. I peered through the window to glimpse a bit of the scattering colorful lights, but I was unlucky. The sounds are very clear, but it was obvious the actions were happening much farther from my immediate community.

My mind can't help but think about how this evening is being celebrated. I dreaded today. Many people are at parties, church meetings, clubs, and other celebratory gatherings, mingling with friends, loved ones, and strangers in order to be with others when the "ball drops." At countdown time, everyone is to look at the person they love in the eye, as tradition dictates, and give a sweet kiss at the striking of midnight!

Naturally, my thoughts traveled to Chris and what he must be doing now. He has found a new person to move on with and I wonder now what they must be doing. I am tempted to be angry, or, if I were rich, hop on a plane and find him, or sit here on my bed and cry. I am actually quite close to doing the latter. One more year is about to begin, and I will again, look at my walls and cry. He, however, gets to be with someone else, even though he is technically still married to me. It's funny how I can never be so "lucky." It gets old after two years. No one wants to greet a new year like this.

Most recently—as recent as this week—I have learnt that I have to move on in spite of my wishes and prayers. In spite of my renewed love for Chris, this journey is quite different and I will have to get used to this new idea pretty soon or I will have a tumultuous ride from here on through.

God and I had a serious heart-to-heart closet talk last night. That is why I am not crying tonight. It is because of what we said to each other and heard from each, that I don't think I will cry. To me, crying would mean that His power is useless and I have given in to the human carnal mind. Last night, He reminded me that he who seeks, finds and he who asks in His name, will be granted as he believes. (Read Matt 7:7 & John 15:7.) I went to bed last night, after hours of crying and pouring out my soul to Him, saying, "It is done. It is done." I believed it and went to sleep.

Saying hello is a great feeling. It means a new experience has come—you can either embrace it or turn it away. Many individuals get excited about this part—It's new, fresh, mysterious, daring, encouraging, challenging, energy-filled, and even crazy. One of the reasons that I feel the way I do now as I write is that last year at this time I was two weeks away from having our newest baby, Elianah. I was checking my hospital bag, my blood pressure, my nerves, my heart, and my budget—all in preparation for our first daughter. I couldn't wait to say hello to her. She was the newest reason for living. My friends and family were all excited.

My God is tender hearted. Michael just came to me and said, "Mom, your bed is warm…and…for both of us." I looked at him, smiled, and then asked, "Do you want to sleep with me tonight?" His face lit up as he said, "Yes!" Then he proceeded to jump into my bed. This is the first time in about two week that he has asked to do this! He loves his new space and went straight to bed at nights without a fuss. It is so sweet. It takes the edge off the loneliness a bit. I'm watching him curled up beside me fast asleep. God is so loving and thoughtful.

I missed Chris terribly as it got closer to my delivery date. I wanted him near for many understandable reasons, but circumstances had it that we were apart. So now, I am reliving the same feeling, only last year I was literally filled with an embodiment of love while yearning for another, and this year I am empty, devoid of both. When I feel like crashing onto the floor, I remember to call upon Jesus. "He shall call upon me, and I will answer him: I will be with him in trouble; I will deliver him, and honour him" (Ps. 91:15).

Mourning the loss of two people I have loved and lost in the same year is an emotion beyond what words can describe. Others have survived worse, like Joy Swift and the loss of her five children. I am glad for her because she had her husband at her side. They carried each other through the horrendous journey. I want to lean, to rest, and to be relieved of many pressures. Human contact, especially from those we hold dearest helps us survive the worst possible circumstances with less anxiety and pressure. It is a marvelous chemistry that keeps us humble in our relationships and helps us to value the existence of others. With all that is in me, I wish Chris was here, but this isn't a fairy tale where genies grant wishes with a poof. Oh wow! I find myself laughing because just the thought of such an instant gratification would blow my mind away. Man, I would just love to run to him and cry until I have had enough. His strong arms were what I have needed for almost two years.

Not being able to see God gives a more sincere appreciation of His power to comfort people like me who are without comforters. The Bible did say that He will never leave us comfortless. (See John 14:18, 26). How can a Person I cannot see be so close that I can walk without falling?

God is God alone, and nothing can match His majesty and regal beauty in character! I see Him more than ever before. If God can hold all the elements of the universe together so that neither you nor I perishes from a slight glitch, then I am quite secure in offering Him my heart and hand. I'd rather be led by no other.

Céline Dion wrote a line in a song: "Goodbye's the saddest word I'll ever hear." She follows this by saying that it will be the last time she will hold her loved one near. "Goodbye" can mean "till then," "later," "gone," "failure," "no more," "a new page," "it is finished" or "never again." There are many reasons we may choose to use this sad word. No one really wants to say "Goodbye." Saying this means that something is bringing about separation of some sort. Another songwriter penned that there will be no goodbyes in Heaven. This makes for a hopeful sermon.

As the music blasts through the walls of the festivities of the old year and the new, people are excited about saying "goodbye," simply because they see the hope of a new "hello;" Even more because they welcome it with the one they hold close as they say "goodbye" to the old year. This makes it a happy—not a sad—occasion.

For me, saying "Goodbye, 2014" evokes much pain. Two major life-changing events occurred this year and 2015 means that I am supposed to turn a new page. Does this new page mean forgetting my baby girl and the love of my life? This is a question that needs careful consideration. I am supposed to say goodbye to the pain and suffering that occurred this year and celebrate the freedom I have from them as the New Year rolls over. This too, is a tricky notion.

Everything has its place, as Solomon emphasizes in Ecclesiastes 3:1[21]. There is no set time frame for grieving. What should matter is that the symbolic representation of the "new year" means that I should grab the opportunity to create a different vision, adjust my lens, and think differently. The tradition works for those who take the new opportunity of the "new year" seriously. At this moment in time, God hears millions of resolutions, or promises of change, ascending up and yonder. Does it create an ambitious moral drive to achieve more? Sure. Yet, we have to be careful that when the month of March dawns on us, we aren't caught flailing because our ideas aren't so novel or exciting anymore. After all, a year contains 365 days, most times. Who bothers to consider the actual length of the upcoming year when making promises?

> *No matter how we may view it, it all ends up being wonderful. We only need to remember that, like a well-made loaf of bread, it will all come to fullness in His time.*

Being a Christian gives the word "goodbye" an additional meaning—one of a more hopeful definition. Christ promises us a life after this one. He promised us an eternity filled with bliss; a life like no script can ever plot. This, my friend, means we will have to say goodbye to this life first. Do you mind the "goodbye" with eternity in view?

Even though I said my "goodbyes" to my three-months-and-a-day-old

---

[21] "To everything there is a season, and a time to every purpose under the heaven:" (Eccles. 3:1).

daughter in May of this year, I am joyful, for I know that the prospect of saying "hello" is near. It is very real as I choose to believe it. God had taken time out to show me that He exists so that I can believe in this hope. "Goodbye" means a new start for Chris and me, whether separately or together. "Goodbye" can mean that, in the future, he and I will return to each other with many old perspectives gone and new ones in view, which would not be a bad idea.

To be in Christ, is to be a new creation; old things have passed away (2 Cor. 5:17). This means that the converted one will have said "goodbye" to a few things. You see, in Christ, there is no dim meaning of anything. Nothing means us harm, and nothing means pain. No matter how we may view it, it all ends up being wonderful. We only need to remember that, like a well-made loaf of bread, it will all come to fullness in His time.

Be encouraged today. I am.

EPILOGUE

Be of good courage, and he shall strengthen your heart, all ye that hope in the Lord. Ps 31:24

Therefore I say unto you, What things soever ye desire, when ye pray, believe that ye receive them, and ye shall have them. Mar 11:24

10 months and 18 days later....

As I sat there on Chris' veranda, I saw the text come in, and I knew what God's answer was before I even picked up the phone. Her timing was especially usual; it was exactly 4:46 AM! She was a powerful praying woman of God, and I knew the kind of experience I was about to have all too well. Though Pat never called to give me a word from the Lord at that hour of the morning, I felt God was about to finalize something. God has been using this woman to speak to me over the past six weeks or so. She would always call when God knew I needed a firm unbiased word. This was one such time.

I had not slept a wink that night, and I was ready to leave his apartment and never return. I made up my mind that I had enough. Chris needed to make a decision and stick with it *(though I already knew what God said would happen, it's the "when" that was unclear).*

> *Pat's phone call and voice note sent me deeper into anguish, because, again, God was clear, "Stay put". I heard Him, but I was tired.*

You see, when Pat called that morning, I was almost at the point of letting go of everything God told me. I was tired of being rejected, exhausted from being vulnerable, wounded from being consistently beaten by marital challenges and discouraged by what was seemingly clear to the human eye. I could not hold on any longer; there was nothing for me to hold to. I felt God was just allowing Satan to beat me just to see how long I could take it without breaking. I couldn't understand why I couldn't get a simple joy in life—having my loving family. Along with being laid off and Chris not being sure if choosing his family was the right and best thing to do, I found out three weeks ago that the surgeon *did* do the tubal ligation while he delivered Elianah. Meaning, I cannot have another child *(at least not in a natural way)*.

Pat's phone call and voice note sent me deeper into anguish, because, again, God was clear, "Stay put". I heard Him, but I was tired. She agonized with God on my behalf over the phone. She begged God to keep me in His bosom and not allow me to lose hope.

With all the crying, we were both not able to speak after a while. We could only sob in silence. Breathing had to be controlled while we silently and reverently prostrated ourselves before the Almighty's throne.

When she was through standing in the gap for us, she asked to pray with Chris separately. I unsteadily took the phone inside to him. He hadn't slept either. Too much was unsaid and overwhelming sadness loomed in the night.

Miraculously, I watched a scene unroll rapidly before my eyes that I will never forget. I had to tell you my story's end to prove how important it is to hold on to God. Never give up! NEVER cease to pray. Pray and fast. Keep on your knees because your battles aren't carnal but spiritual.

> *In June of this year, God said to me, through the voice of a complete stranger, "Live in the already, though it is not yet".*

Chris told me after the prayer that his is not ending our marriage, and he communicated that to the other woman before I entered the room. I expected no such thing—at least not now. I was so surprised I couldn't speak for a while. When the phone calls kept coming in, he repeatedly reaffirmed his decision to stick with his family and I was a witness. It was awestriking and humbling to hear the divine revelations being confirmed through Chris' speech to me. God had shown me not to live by sight but faith in the Word.

God is powerful friends, and anything is possible in Christ! The reconciliation, through relieving, came with stinging tears, bold confessions and the realization that we wasted many years. However, know this, we are all being fashioned according to the similitude of our perfect Heavenly Father, and His lessons are in stages. Decide to learn and keep climbing.

After the breakthrough and revelations, this happened. At 5:22 AM on November 18, 2015, a WhatsApp text came in. It read: "Because thine heart was tender, and thou hast humbled thyself before the Lord, when thou heardest what I spake against this place, and against the inhabitants thereof, that they should become a desolation and a curse, and hast rent thy clothes, and wept before me; I also have heard thee, saith the Lord." (2 Kings 22:19.) Pat sent it. She sent it without knowing what took place after she hung up from praying. See what I mean? Powerful!

> God answered my constant petition to save my family and restore the lost years. He is willing to do the same for you.

In June of this year, God said to me, through the voice of a complete stranger, "Live in the already, though it is not yet". God instructed me to honour His word on marriage, and He will honour me. What a kind Saviour! Chris and I are now reconciled and not like in a popular movie scene or how people determined. We were finally reconciled when the work that needed to be done was completed, when specific steps were made and when we both yielded selflessly to the Holy Spirit.

God answered my constant petition to save my family and restore the lost years. He is willing to do the same for you. He sent messengers and signs my way to encourage me to "stay put". Be alert. Your signs are there as well. Open your eyes and stay connected to the Life Giver.

Through it all, hold on to the Promise. Through all the messy experiences and the blinding pain, hold on to the Peace Speaker. Why? God is He who sits on the throne, then and now. Be a witness! Our Almighty God and Creator is in control.

...~~And they lived happily ever after~~

…And with God, all things continue to be possible.

We invite you to view the complete
selection of titles we publish at:

www.ASPECTBooks.com

Scan with your mobile
device to go directly
to our website.

Please write or email us your praises, reactions,
or thoughts about this or any other book we publish at:

P.O. Box 954
Ringgold, GA 30736

info@ASPECTBookscom

ASPECT Books titles may be purchased in bulk for
educational, business, fund-raising, or sales promotional use.
For information, please e-mail:

BulkSales@ASPECTBooks.com

Finally, if you are interested in seeing
your own book in print, please contact us at

publishing@ASPECTBooks.com

We would be happy to review your manuscript for free.

www.ingramcontent.com/pod-product-compliance
Lightning Source LLC
Chambersburg PA
CBHW080553170426
43195CB00016B/2779